T0384885

What Every Engineer Should Know About

Microcomputer Program Design

WHAT EVERY ENGINEER SHOULD KNOW
A Series

Editor

William H. Middendorf

Department of Electrical and Computer Engineering
University of Cincinnati
Cincinnati, Ohio

Other volumes in preparation

What Every Engineer Should Know About
Microcomputer Program Design

Keith R. Wehmeyer
Cincinnati Milacron
Cincinnati, Ohio

MARCEL DEKKER, INC.   New York and Basel

Library of Congress Cataloging in Publication Data

Wehmeyer, Keith, [date]
   What every engineer should know about
microcomputer program design.

   (What every engineer should know ; v. 14)
   Includes index.
   1. Microcomputers--Programming. 2. Structured
programming.   I. Title. II. Series.
QA76.6.W435   1984   001.64'2   84-12052
ISBN 0-8247-7275-X

MARCEL DEKKER, INC.
270 Madison Avenue, New York, New York 10016

Current Printing (last digit):
10 9 8 7 6 5 4 3 2 1

PRINTED IN THE UNITED STATES OF AMERICA

PREFACE

The computer has become the single most powerful problem – solving tool in today's technically minded world. Whether it is a pocket calculator or a large mainframe, the computer offers the ability to perform complicated, tedious tasks with great speed and efficiency. The birth and continued development of the microprocessor has made computing power available at reasonable cost to the home and small business.

A new problem therefore results: that of programming the computer to get the desired operations to perform properly. This book presents the concept of Structured Program Design, a systematic way to create computer programs efficiently. This method begins with an assessment of the problem and continues through the development, coding, and testing of the computer program. Built into this system is a method of programming that makes additions, enhancements, or corrections much easier to implement as the program undergoes revisions. The book is intended for two audiences: beginning programmers and experienced programmers seeking ways to improve the quality of their software. Structured Program Design techniques provide an excellent way for novice programmers to "think through" a problem until they arrive at a working solution. Advanced programmers in general do not presently use methods to improve coding efficiency or readability, areas where these techniques are of great help.

This book covers the entire scope of computer programming and Structured Program Design, from problem identification to maintaining existing programs. Chapter 1 presents a general overview of the Structured Program Design process, with subsequent chapters detailing each phase. An example is carried out through the book to show how each phase is implemented. An unusual feature of this book is that all the techniques presented here will work on a variety of computers that use many different languages. Thus, these techniques work as well on programmable calculators as they do on large business computers. The objective is still the same: to write programs that efficiently produce reliable output and are easy to use and understand.

Other supplemental areas of programming are covered such as a software library, programming personnel, and program documentation. These areas are often overlooked but play a key part in organizations with an ongoing programming effort.

I wish to express my thanks to Dr. William H. Middendorf, Professor of Electrical Engineering, University of Cincinnati, for his advice and editorial suggestions. My wife Jannis has been invaluable, both with her encouragement and typing skills. I am also indebted to my brother Stephen for his excellent artwork. And finally, a thank you to my entire family, whose support made this work possible.

Enjoy the book! I hope it makes your programs easier to write and maintain by reducing the headaches and late nights along the way.

Keith R. Wehmeyer

CONTENTS

        Requirements Analysis   20
        Sources of Requirements   20
        Ranking of Requirements   22
        Traits of a Good Program   25
        An Example   29
        Program MENU   31
        Program INPUT   33
        Program REPORTS   36
        Additional Specification   39
        References   42

3 SOFTWARE DESIGN   45

        Determination of Resources   45
        Choosing the Language   47
        Design Techniques   49
        Flow Charts   53
        Psuedo Code   58
        The Project Workbook   59
        The Design Review   60
        Summary   61
        Flow Chart Examples   62

4 CODING AND DEBUGGING SOFTWARE   67

        Flow Chart Conversions to Program Code   68
        Types of Documentation   69
        The Structured Walk-Through   72

Contents

ABOUT THE AUTHOR

Keith R. Wehmeyer is currently employed as a
Research Engineer in the Software Development group
of the Robot Research department at Cincinnati
Milacron Industries Inc., Cincinnati, Ohio. He is
responsible for the hardware and software
development of new robot control architectures. He
received the B.S. degree in Electrical Engineering
from the University of Cincinnati in 1982, and is
currently pursuing a Masters of Science degree in
Computer Engineering.

What Every Engineer Should Know About

Microcomputer Program Design

1

AN INTRODUCTION TO
MICROCOMPUTER PROGRAM DESIGN

This chapter presents a complete overview of
microcomputer program design, with key topics
presented in more detail in subsequent chapters. In
addition, a structured technique used in writing
programs is presented as it pertains to structured
program design. This technique will be discussed
throughout the following chapters, as it is the
basis for good program design. Finally, the titles
and responsibilities of several important people in
any programming organization are discussed. We

begin now with a discussion of what microcomputer
program design is and why it should be used.

STRUCTURED PROGRAM DESIGN

Structured program design (SPD) is a systematic
procedure used to create, test, and verify computer
software. As in any other design procedure, the
programmer works through a sequence of pre-planned
steps until the project is completed. This
technique offers many advantages to those who use
it fully, some of which are as follows:

   Efficiency. The programmer who proceeds under
      any set of defined guidelines should produce
      code quicker and with fewer errors. This
      reduces costs and can prevent many of the
      difficulties that will be discussed later in
      this book. As an example, Daly (1) conducted
      a study that compared software (any computer
      program) and hardware (the physical parts of
      a computer) projects of nearly equal
      complexity. His results showed that the
      software project took twice as long and cost
      four times as much to design and maintain as
      the hardware project. He attributed a large
      part of this increased time and cost to the
      fact that the hardware engineers used a more
      systematic approach toward design.

   Maintenance. It is widely accepted that about
      75 - 80% of the programmer´s time is spent
      maintaining existing corporate software.

Software maintenance differs from hardware maintenance in that software is "repaired" in order to correct errors or add functions, instead of fixing a system that no longer functions correctly. By using good design techniques, the programmer can free himself to spend more time on new design challenges. In addition, a program written using structured program techniques will be much easier to understand and modify.

Cost Reduction. Hardware costs drop a factor of ten every decade, so an increasing amount of a project's total cost will depend on software generation. While the programmer may not be able to boost productivity at the same rate, any improvement will have an increasingly significant effect in controlling cost.

Unfortunately, many programmers do not use guidelines, and few are learning to use them. In a study by McClure (2), the results pointed to the fact that most programmers had not changed their approach to programming in the last five years and had no plans to do so in the next five. Thus, a great deal of improvement is possible by following only the simplest of guidelines.

PARALLELS WITH ENGINEERING DESIGN

Virtually every engineer is familiar with the engineering method of design. This basic approach stems from the scientific method, which is comprised of the following steps:

1. Observe a phenomenon.
2. Postulate a theory to explain the occurence of the phenomenon.
3. Construct a test to prove the theory.
4. Draw conclusions as to the validity of the theory based on the test results.

The engineering method parallels this with the following steps:

1. Recognize and specify a need.
2. Specify a product to fill the need.
3. Design the product according to the above specification.
4. Verify that the product design meets the specifications and fills the need.

Note that all four steps in the engineering method could be used to construct a program. Ideally, a specification should first be written based on a set of requirements. Next, a design process should be used to create and debug a program. Finally, the program should be checked against the specification for accuracy and completeness.

Other steps should be included in the software design process as well. Since most programs undergo frequent revisions and modifications, a convenient way of recording and documenting changes should be included. In addition, user documentation should be prepared, such as instruction or operation manuals. This documentation is very important, since it may be the only link between the program´s authors and users.

THE EIGHT STEPS OF STRUCTURED PROGRAM DESIGN

As previously stated, many of the steps used in other forms of engineering design are found in program design. Myers (3) summarizes the work of software generation into the following eight steps:

1. Requirements Analysis and Definition. This is the point where the user and the authors begin the design process by deciding what they wish to do with a given configuration of hardware. Notice that the function of the program is to control the hardware in an agreed-upon fashion.

2. Specification. At this point the desires of all parties are put into written form and are concretely defined. Time and cost limits are to be established and detailed as well. Since the specification will be referred to throughout the rest of the design process, the creation of a clear, well - defined specification is essential. This is usually the last point where a user´s input is considered until the program is operational.

3. Design. Once the program specification is done, the programmer then begins to determine what resources will be required. Following this, construction of a project workbook begins. This workbook should contain the specification and all other materials used in the project. Next, the program logic is contructed using one of several design techniques into a flow chart of operation. This flow chart can be one that uses actual code, English phrases, or symbols to denote what the program will do and when.

4. Programming. Once the program's logic has been charted, it is up to the programmer to convert the flow chart into actual program code. Included in this conversion should be documentation showing the "how and why" of program operation. In essence, the flow chart statements are placed next to the code that performs the corresponding functions. Following this, a structured "walk-through" review of the program is suggested as an error-trapping mechanism before the program is entered into a machine. The scope and function of the structured walk-through is discussed later in this book. Finally, the testing and debugging process continues inside the machine until the program functions as its author believes it should. It is in this phase that most proponents of structured

program   design   techniques   feel   the
greatest   amounts   of   time,   money,   and
energy are saved.

5.   Verification and Testing. Once the program
is operating in the machine, it must be
checked   against   the   specification   for
accuracy and correctness. Programs   not
meeting the   specification will repeat the
design process   once   again   from   the
beginning and will   not pass this step
until   the   program fulfills the specified
need. Once this is so, the program must
then   be tested thoroughly for   reliability
under conditions that any user is expected
to   have. Finally,   the program   must be
tested under adverse conditions to make
sure the program protects both itself and
its data from errors and erroneous input
by   the   user. Such "bullet-proof" testing
cannot be exhaustive in large systems,
such as a multi-user operating system. In
fact, it may not be possible to simulate
all possible errors or modes of operation
within a reasonable amount of time. In
this case, the programmer must choose the
most probable errors.

6.   Performance Appraisal. At this point the
program   is   considered   functionally
acceptable and further information must be
gathered as   to its characteristics. Here
the   program   is evaluated on its   quality

and efficient use of resources such as
outside equipment, time, and memory. The
software is also evaluated as to its
flexibility, clarity, and its ability to
be used in other machines or situations
(known as portability and adaptability).
Finally, the program is checked to see if
changes and modifications can be added
easily without major revisions. If an area
is found unacceptable, the programmer
should take steps to optimize those areas
so the software will function properly.
Another review should then be done against
the specification in these areas, as they
should be within the scope of a user´s
requirements. This step differs from the
preceding ones since the programmer shifts
emphasis from design to optimization and
compression.

7. Operation and Maintenance. As previously
   stated, a programmer spends close to 75%
   of his time in the function of
   maintenance. In this step, the operations
   and instruction manuals are prepared and
   minor revisions are made to aid the
   operator in using the software. Errors
   that have managed to get through the
   various stages of testing are corrected
   here. Since users are not always
   programmers (they may be businesspeople,
   secretaries, or engineers), care must be

taken to make sure they can learn how to
use the program in the shortest possible
time period and with the least amount of
assistance from outside sources.

8. Configuration Management. Finally, a method
of documenting changes and informing users
of this act is needed. Revisions which are
desired by users are processed through
change notices, repetition of the above
design steps, and documentation of the
problem and its solution. This leads to
the release of new or modified software.
This software must somehow be
distinguished from previous versions and
should include any new applicable
instructions. The new software must also
be stored so future access is guaranteed
for subsequent changes.

Not all programmers need to use every step
described above; some may use more, some less. Some
may even differ in how the project is divided. The
technique presented above is only a small subset of
the many methods available to design programs in a
structured fashion. The important thing is that a
standard technique should be used that will tell
the programmer what needs to be done and when. Such
techniques help in the initial design effort and
will guarantee less confusion when changes are to
be made at a later date.

THE CONCEPT OF MODULARITY

Computer programs often become so large that a
programmer could not keep track of all the
functions at one time. When this situation occurs,
the programmer is forced to break the functions up
into small groups and work on each group
separately. This "divide and conquer" technique is
called modular decomposition.

Modular decomposition has the advantage of the
programmer being able to concentrate his efforts on
one individual problem without worrying about
others. In addition, several programmers can each
tackle one problem simultaneously and then combine
their efforts into a finished program. To use this
technique, the programmer simply divides the
program into groups (commonly called modules), and
assigns someone to program and test each module.
When complete, the modules are chained together
into the finished program.

Modules are usually grouped by a common
function or process. Examples of this would be a
module which handles all I/O (input/output) using
the keyboard and display screen, a module which
adds two numbers to it and returns the result, and
a module that diagnoses errors and informs the
users of any problems. Note from Figure 1.1 that
modules are characterized by a single entry point
where data is supplied, a process which acts upon
the data given to yield a result, and a single exit
point which returns the result to the calling

program. In addition, these modules can then be
broken down further into smaller modules if
necessary. An example of this is a program which
utilizes one module to handle math functions and is
comprised of smaller modules which divide,
multiply, subtract, etc. These modules can in turn
be broken down into smaller modules which will
eventually lead to a module small enough to be
transformed into code easily.

REASONS FOR MODULAR DECOMPOSITION

As stated before, modular programming allows the
use of multiple programmers who can each focus
their attention on one specific problem and solve
it. When finished, the modules can be grouped

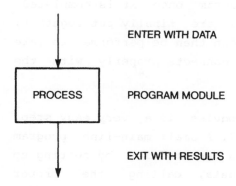

ENTER WITH DATA

PROCESS   PROGRAM MODULE

EXIT WITH RESULTS

FIGURE 1.1

together to form the finished program. However,
other advantages can be obtained by programming
this way.

Since all modules are independent, they can be
re-used in other programs that require the same
function. Thus, a module need only be written once
and then copied for use in other programs. By
keeping a catalog of all modules, the programmer
can re-use his own and other´s work instead of
re-creating identical software. This will reduce
the time and expense of generating future programs.

Since modules are written separately due to
their independence, they can be tested separately
for the same reason. Each module can be tested for
accuracy and completeness simply by verifying that
acceptable data returns from the module based on
the data supplied. Troubleshooting on such a small
scale is easier and more thorough than attempting
to test the entire program once it is completed.
When the program modules are finally put together,
a simpler system test can then be performed to make
sure that each module connects properly with the
next one.

Linking all the modules is a very easy step,
as shown in Figure 1.2. A small main-line program
is created that groups the modules by setting up
the necessary input data, calling the proper
module, and then using that module´s results for
either another module or as data to be supplied to
the user. This main-line program takes very little

time to code and requires less time to debug, since
each   of   the   modules   are   tested   separately
beforehand.

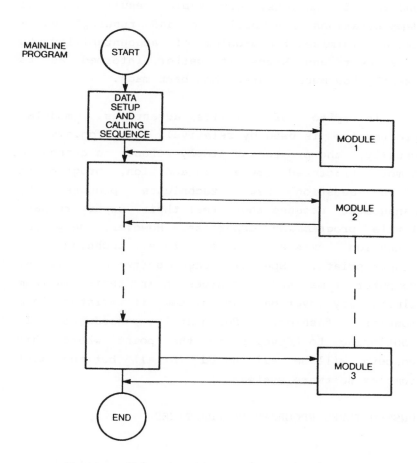

FIGURE 1.2

Finally, this method allows programmers to relate their progress to their superiors in a meaningful manner. Management is more pleased to see a module in operation (even if it is only one small part of the total package) than it is to see an entire program coded on sheets they do not understand. Obvious, observable results such as demonstrations of a module "up and running" on a system minimizes the problem of accountability to management and keeps it better informed as to exactly how much progress has been made.

In spite of all its advantages, modular programming is used by relatively few programmers. Usually, the programmer simply refuses to change to a more structured style. In addition, programmers often question new techniques proposed by management because they feel their superiors have little programming expertise. However, only one situation exists where this technique is inappropriate. Special case software utilizing computer time and resources near their maximum limits may overload the system if written in a modular fashion. Fortunately, hardware is continuing to develop to the point where this concern will be eliminated in all but the most complex software systems.

UNSTRUCTURED PROGRAMMING PRACTICES

In contrast to the step-by-step method of structured program design, many individuals continue to program in an unstructured fashion. Their programming method usually begins with the same input from users, but has quite a different ending.

Rather than write a specification on the program, the programmer usually takes notes in one form or another. This causes confusion because the user and the programmer have no real documentation that details what the program should do. Thus, the user's desires are not clearly outlined and are usually not implemented correctly.

The programmer then begins to write the program by directly keying it in to the computer, organizing and constructing the program flow as he goes. As a result, most of the program is a straight-line routine which has no shared modules and wastes a great deal of space. Since the flow chart of operation is not done, no attempt is made to optimize each operation for efficiency. Often the program is written with no comments included, adding further to confusion at a later date when changes are required.

The verification and testing process is done by running the program and solving each program "bug" as it appears. Often this causes errors in other parts of the program related to the one being corrected without the programmer's knowledge. The unstructured program becomes even worse, as the

patching process continues to get the program to
function. This oftens riddles the program with
errors, which will require many hours of additional
time to correct later. Thus, the programmer
releases a defective piece of software to the user,
forgets about it, and then spends a great deal of
time attempting to remember how each operation was
performed when the errors are found. This also
wastes the programmer´s time, as he is no longer
writing new software, but is tied up in maintaining
a program with only his memory as the source of
documentation. All in all, this method is extremely
inefficient and time consuming, especially during
the maintenance cycle throughout the rest of the
program´s life. In addition, this also requires
that a new programmer spend considerable amounts of
time becoming familiar with a program before he can
make changes to it or understand it.

KEY INDIVIDUALS IN PROGRAM DESIGN

In this chapter we have reviewed many of the steps
used in structured program design. The
responsibility for the completion of most of these
steps has been placed on the programmer, but there
are several other individuals who assist in this
procedure.

    One of the most important people in a
programming organization is the librarian who
catalogs, dates, and files all the completed
modules and stores the documentation covering them.
In this way, all programmers have access to the

complete collection of modules for possible re-use.
Changes, revisions, and enhancements are also kept
on file along with the original program. Thus, the
librarian is able to provide the complete history
of a given module from its origin to its last
revision, with a complete description and dates of
all changes. This information allows new
programmers to become familiar with a certain
module and allows those who have forgotten parts of
its operation a chance to refresh their memories.
Utilizing a librarian and some form of storage is
essential when many authors contribute software
that will be available to a large group of users.

Another important person in the software
design process is the chief programmer. This
individual co-ordinates the activities of all
programmers as they work on a project in the same
manner that an engineering manager controls
technical personnel under his supervision. Chief
programmers usually conduct progress report
meetings and are responsible for scheduling work.
In addition, the chief programmer is a source of
company resources and information, and is usually
the first person to provide help to the programmer.
Thus, the chief programmer functions as both a
manager and as a programmer, providing the
necessary link between management and staff.

In most companies, neither of these positions
require full time personnel. The librarian may be a
programmer whose job duties have been expanded to
include program storage for his lab group. In some

cases, the department or laboratory head may assume the duties of chief programmer in addition to other responsibilities. Remember, the important points are that these functions are defined and assigned to one individual and that the other programmers recognize this fact. In this way, the programmer knows where to go to borrow or save software and to whom progress reports should be made.

REFERENCES

1. Edmund B. Daly , Management of Software Development , IEEE Transactions in Software Engineering, May 1977, pp. 229 - 242.

2. Robert M. McClure, Software - The Next Five Years, Digest of Papers, COMPCON Spring 1976, pp. 6-7.

3. Ware Myers, The Need for Software Engineering, Computer, February 1978, p 15.

2

REQUIREMENTS ANALYSIS
AND SPECIFICATION

This chapter contains an in-depth look at the first
steps in program design: the requirements analysis
and specification. In these steps the desires of
users and programmers are written down into a clear
and concise specification which will be referred to
during the rest of the design process. Many of the
decisions and trade-offs used by the programmers
will come from their interpretation of this
specification. Therefore, successful completion of
these two steps is essential to the continued
development of good software.

REQUIREMENTS ANALYSIS

Before any problem can be solved by using these
techniques, it must be defined properly.
Comprehension of the scope and limits of a problem
can go a long way in finding its eventual solution.
In fact, understanding and defining the problem may
be just as difficult as solving it.

One of the best ways to define a software
program is to arrive at the program's functions. By
generating a list of what operations the user
expects the program to perform, the program can be
defined. These requirements are then grouped
together to form a functional or performance
specification. It should be obvious that as each
function is described in greater detail, the
program itself becomes better defined. Ideally, all
the functions should be included as requirements so
that the number of decisions made by the programmer
is minimized.

SOURCES OF REQUIREMENTS

When deciding what operations a program must
perform, the user is the most likely source of
ideas. Computer operators will usually request
program performance that is easy to understand and
requires a minimum of training to use. In addition,
most prefer that the program is "friendly"; that
is, the computer interacts with the user in a

"human" fashion when it requires decision making or data. It is also desirable to have the program point out and recover from bad data inputs by the user, such as wrong numbers or incorrect spelling. Finally, the user wants this program to be less time consuming than the method currently used to provide the same function.

Another source of requirements is the other programmers. Since their role in the program continues as the program is changed or modified, it is useful to make the program modular so changes can be made easily. It is also necessary for the program code to include documentation on the function of each module, so someone other than the programmer can understand or recall its operation at a later date. Programmers are also concerned about using a minimum amount of memory space and computer time, especially on machines that have many jobs running at the same time. Since new computers are replacing older, more outdated models continuously, it is usually desirable to write programs so they may be used on more than one machine. The reader should note that programmers place more emphasis on requirements which make the next steps in program design easier, rather than concern themselves with how the program interacts with users. Programmers must also deal with the limits imposed by the computer, since few users will have much knowledge about their machines.

A final source of requirements can come from management. It is not uncommon for a request to be

made to duplicate an existing program written by
another company so that it can be used on a
different computer or in a different way. Having
received input in some form of a user´s survey,
modifications may be ordered to improve the program
into a marketable product. Management may also
authorize programmers to write programs that
perform new functions if they believe a need exists
which these programs could fill.

RANKING OF REQUIREMENTS

When the individuals desiring the program or others
interested in it arrive at a decision about what
functions should be included, the programmer should
meet with them to begin ranking the requirements.
Unless the programmer is writing the program for
private use, each individual should include their
"wish list" and participate in the ranking
procedure. Input from sales, programming,
maintenance, and the final users should be
considered and weighed accordingly. In this way,
the desires of each group are known and a
compromise can be reached that is satisfactory to
everyone. This helps to eliminate the problem that
arises when the end user tells the programmers that
the project they have spent six months on is "not
what was wanted."

There are many ways requirements can be ranked
to form a specification, several of which will be
discussed here. One simple method is commonly used
in other forms of engineering design. This

technique can be used just as effectively on software design. In this procedure, each desire is assigned one of three classes, depending upon its necessity. These classes are:

1. Requirement. A software feature assigned the weight of a requirement must be included in the final program design. A requirement is usually rigid and most design decisions and trade-offs will center about it. Examples of requirements would be the minimum set of functions the program must perform and limits imposed on memory size. Note that requirements are measureable features which can be verified by testing the completed software.

2. Goals. A feature with the weighting of a goal is not as important or inflexible as a requirement. Goals tend to apply to the "finishing touches" of a program, representing ideal operations or the most versatility. Examples of goals include development time limits, formats for interaction with the user, and desires for easy modification and adaptation.

3. Preference. A software feature weighted as a preference carries the minimum amount of inflexibility. Trade-offs made to accomodate requirements usually result in the change or removal of some preferences. The most desirable method chosen from a

group of several acceptable methods is
normally ranked as a preference. Since
there is usually more than one alternative
to the preference, the programmer has the
greatest flexibility in these areas.

Once each of the software features and desires
has been ranked as a requirement, goal, or
preference, the final specification can then be
written. First, the requirements are included and
their impact on other areas is reviewed. Next, the
goals are written in as they pertain to the
requirements, suggesting approaches and defining
limits. Finally, the preferences are included to
show areas where alternate choices could be used in
case problems are discovered. The final
specification should then cover all major areas of
program operation with a minimum of ambiguity
concerning what should be included in the program.
In this way the programmer concerns himself more
with the actual design and implementation of the
subroutines and modules in the later design stages,
since most of the general program layout is
designed here.

Another method of requirements analysis
centers upon topics common to all programs. A group
of common characteristics such as program speed and
size, data storage, and use of peripherals is
agreed upon first. With these characteristics as a
guideline, the program is then described according
to those characteristics (uses small memory size,
requires large data storage, needs terminal or

keyboard as peripherals, etc.). Each description is then given a weighting (a suggested weight is from 1 to 10) concerning how necessary it is for the program to have that characteristic. One example of this would be the characteristic of execution time, the description that this must be minimized to a level beneath some maximum value, and a suitable weighting given to the description that provides some measure of how necessary this condition is. In some cases a characteristic may have no importance at all when compared to another program. For example, the speed at which the computer updates the display screen is not critical when used in a program that computes the slope of a line; while simulation of moving objects, such as those used in computer aided design, requires display updates at a frequent enough rate to cause flicker-free operation. By reviewing these rankings, the programmer is able to find areas where trade-offs can be used to arrive at the final program.

TRAITS OF A GOOD PROGRAM

When specifying a program according to its characteristics or determining its requirements, goals, and preferences, the following traits should be considered. While this list is not complete, it represents many of the concerns that should be studied and included as part of the specification. A good program:

    1. Works according to specification. Part of any specification should include a review

of the program where evaluation and acceptance tests are performed. Those who decided upon the specification should ensure that the final, released version includes all the features that were intended.

2. Is done on time. Completing a project by a realistic time limit is accomplished by using a standard program design technique where limits are set for each phase of the project. Techniques such as the Project Evaluation and Review Technique (PERT) and Critical Path Monitoring (CPM) are helpful in setting time limits for each project phase and pointing out areas where completion by a set time is critical.

3. Is simple. Good programmers use the most simple, easy-to-understand algorithms in solving computer problems. The simpler the program is, the easier it is to maintain and change. No extra credit is awarded to programmers who include all the necessary functions in the program but do so in a way that is inflexible or is impossible to comprehend.

4. Is well structured. The benefits of using modular programming techniques have been discussed earlier, supporting the claim that modular programs out-perform others in many different ways. A well-structured

program implies simplicity of organization to complement the simplicity discussed above in the actual implementation. Programs with clearly labeled modules are much easier to understand when viewed for the first time, and make the process of refreshing the memory of the original author a much quicker task.

5. Is efficient. A computer program is judged to be efficient when it requires the minimum user interaction, uses the computer and its peripherals for the least amount of time, and generates the smallest number of clear pages of output data. For companies that must hire help to operate their computer systems or must use outside computing services, this characteristic is a must. Many times the deciding factor in whether a business can afford a computer is the amount of work that a present employee can get done and how much time will be saved over present methods.

6. Is cost effective. Programs that engineers may write and then market should be prepared at reasonable cost and should be priced in a manner that reflects the utility provided. Programs prepared by a company for its own use should be general enough so they can be adapted for use in other situations to recover development costs.

7. Is changeable. Since programs are being
    changed continually, the initial design
    should be done with revisions in mind. It
    is helpful if a program is written to
    allow for expansions, revisions, and
    modifications. A recent study by the
    General Motors Corporation (1) found that
    75% of their software work was done on
    maintaining existing programs. If programs
    are written to allow for continued
    maintenance, this problem will be
    minimized and allow for more time to be
    spent on new projects.

8. Is well documented. None of the changes,
    maintenance, or improvements can be
    implemented if documentation is not
    provided that will assist the programmer
    in discovering how the program functions.
    At the end of each revision, documentation
    should also be prepared to explain what
    changes were made and where they were
    inserted. This documentation should be
    thorough enough that another programmer
    can resume development should the original
    author be unavailable. Documentation
    should also be prepared for the user in
    the form of instruction manuals and
    operating guides, with patches provided as
    new revisions are available.

While this list is not comprehensive, careful
consideration of each of these topics will aid in

forming a complete and clear specification that covers the entire operation of the program. If other points seem important and may have some impact on the quality of your programs, include them into specifications and consider them for future specifications on related projects.

AN EXAMPLE

The following example will be carried throughout the remainder of this book, with each step in the SPD process being implemented as it is presented in subsequent chapters. Finally, a working program written in BASIC will be presented, since this language is one of the easiest to understand. Note that this example could be implemented in any level of code, from assembly language (representation of machine code instructions) to high level languages such as PASCAL and FORTRAN. We begin the example with a problem description and (using requirements analysis) will generate a specification covering the entire program's operation.

Consider the following problem. An organization wishes to store information about its members in a data base file. The computer will then take this data and generate printouts of such things as mailing lists and labels, membership cards, and membership rosters. After meeting with the group's officers, it is determined that the following information is to be stored for each member:

First and last name
Street address
City, state, and zip code
Date they first became a member
Yearly dues status (paid/not paid)
Telephone number

The following printouts will also be required:

List of each member´s name, address, and phone
    number
List of all members who have not paid yearly
    membership dues
List of names and addresses for mailing labels
Letter to advise members of the next meeting´s
    location and time
Letter to advise members who are delinquent in
    dues payment

These listings should include headings where
applicable and should prompt the user when data is
required. The last three printouts should also
include the feature that allows printouts of the
entire membership or individual members, one at a
time.

At this point we will now group the entire
operation into two sections. The first section
allows for adding new members to the group,
changing the old data in an existing member´s file,
and removing the file of a departing member. The
second section generates all the reports required.

Moreover, these sections should be separated into
two distinct programs with a third program that
informs the user of all options available, and then
jumps to either of the two programs based on the
user´s request. This program is known as the main
menu, since it shows all options available to the
user. For clarity we will call the main menu
program MENU, the reports printout program REPORTS,
and the membership file entry program INPUT. The
master file which contains all the data about each
member will be named MEMBER/DAT. We may now begin
using requirements analysis to specify each of the
three programs and generate a specification.

PROGRAM MENU

We now detail the operation of program MENU and
assign the value of requirement (R), goal (G), or
preference (P) as detailed in section 2.3. Table
2.1 shows the results of this operation.

TABLE 2.1
Ranking Table of Program MENU

Function of Menu	Ranking
1. Displays all options from both programs on screen	R
2. Prompts user for selection of either program or to exit program in a user friendly manner	R

TABLE 2.1 (continued)

3. Loads and executes the proper program   R
    based on user´s request

4. Rejects bad input by user   G

5. Executes quickly   P

6. Uses minimal memory   P

7. Prompts user in a friendly manner   R

The specification of MENU is then written to
summarize all requirements and indicate the degree
of freedom left to the programmer.

Specification of Program MENU

   Program MENU is the main menu and is executed
first when a user wishes to access the membership
file. This program should be display screen
oriented with user input coming from the keyboard.
This main menu should display the functions of the
programs INPUT and REPORTS and then prompts the
user to request the desired program. MENU will then
load and execute the desired program or warn the
user if an input error has been made. An option to
terminate further operation should also be included
so that the user can return to the operating system
of the computer. The screen format should be clear
and easy to read, but its actual format is left to

the programmer. It is also recommended for the program to execute as quickly as possible and to use the least amount of memory, even though this program should be short enough to be well within limits.

Note that while this specification is not lengthy because the program´s operation is not complex, equally simple programs could have much more detailed specifications. Detailing the specification to any greater extent would remove virtually all design decisions made by the programmer. However, the specification of programs INPUT and REPORT will require much more detail, since they are the heart of the program.

PROGRAM INPUT

We now repeat the design process for the program INPUT, which takes the data supplied by the user and stores it in the membership file.

TABLE 2.2
Ranking Table of Program INPUT

Function of INPUT	Ranking
1. Displays all input functions on the screen (add, change, delete members)	R
2. Prompts user for selection of input function or return to program MENU	R

TABLE 2.2 (continued)

3. ADD function accepts all data and creates   R
    new data record in membership file

4. CHANGE function accepts all data and   R
    substitutes for old data found in record

5. DELETE function removes member from   R
    membership file

6. Screen format and order of input for ADD   G
    and CHANGE should be the same for
    consistency

7. Allows user to start over if an error has   G
    been made in ADD or CHANGE mode

8. Reacts with user in a friendly manner   G

9. Recovers from errors in such a way as to   G
    protect the membership file from becoming
    unusable

10. Uses minimal memory   P

11. Executes quickly   P

12. Termination of each ADD, CHANGE, or   P
    DELETE command returns to INPUT sub-menu

Specification of Program INPUT

Program INPUT is the data entry program which
is called up by the user from program MENU when it
is desired to alter the information stored in the
master file MEMBER/DAT. This program should be
screen oriented and accept user input from the
keyboard. The options available to the user are:

1. ADD a new member to the file
2. CHANGE the data of a current member
3. DELETE the data of an inactive member

The ADD option creates a new record in the
MEMBER/DAT file and allows the user to enter all
the pertinent information about a member. This
information consists of the member´s first and last
name, current address (including city, state, and
zip code), date of membership, phone number
(including area code), and yearly dues status. The
user then enters this data and can review it before
it is stored into the master file. Should an error
exist, the user may re-start and enter the data
again. Once the data is saved or the user desires
to exit, the program returns to the INPUT sub-menu.

The CHANGE option permits the user to access
the record of any member by supplying the record
number. Once a record has been selected, the user
may alter the data contained in it or leave it
alone and go to another record.

If changes are made, the user has the option
to store those changes and proceed or to cancel
those changes and enter new ones. When the user no

longer wants to review or change a member´s record,
the program returns to the INPUT sub-menu.

The DELETE option allows the user to remove
the record of any member from the file. The user
supplies the record number of the member to be
deleted and the program will prompt the user to
verify that this record is to be deleted. If it is
to be deleted, the program removes the record and
exits to the INPUT sub-menu.

PROGRAM REPORTS

Finally, we determine the function and
specification of the third program, REPORTS.
Remember, this program was to generate various
listings from the data stored in the master
membership file MEMBER/DAT.

TABLE 2.3
Ranking Table for Program REPORTS

Function of REPORTS	Ranking
1. Displays sub-menu showing all report printout functions on the screen	R
2. Prompts user for selection of printout function or exit to MENU	R
3. Compiles membership list containing each member´s name, address, and phone number	R

4. Compiles listing of all members who have   R
    not paid yearly dues

5. Prints mailing labels for each active member   R
    showing name and address

6. Prints form letter to members advising time   R
    and place of next meeting

7. Print form letter to members who have not   R
    paid dues to inform them that their payment
    is due

8. Specifications 6 and 7 should allow for   G
    printout of a varying number of copies of
    each letter

9. Form letters used in specification 6 and 7   G
    should be easy to change

10. Form letters in specifications 6 and 7   R
    should prompt for information required at
    time of execution

11. Report formats should be clear and easy   G
    to read

12. Compiling and printing of data should   G
    execute as quickly as possible

13. Program should verify that printer is at   P
    top of form before printing

TABLE 2.3 (Continued)

14. Printouts should fit on 8 1/2 x 11 paper   P

_____

Specification of Program REPORTS

    Program REPORTS is the report printing program
which is called up by the user from program MENU
when printouts of the information contained in
MEMBER/DAT are desired. This program is screen
oriented and accepts user input from the keyboard.
The   resulting printouts are then sent to the
computer´s printer. The options available to the
user are:

    1.   Membership list
    2.   List of members with delinquent dues for
         the year
    3.   Mailing label printouts
    4.   Form letter to notify each member about the
         next meeting
    5.   Form letter advising members that they must
         pay their yearly dues

Report options 4 and 5 can be printed as many times
as needed for the entire group or for selected
individuals of the user´s choice.

    The   membership list prints the   names,
addresses, and phone numbers of all active members
in the group. The delinquent dues list prints the
name of all members who have not paid   their

required yearly dues. The mailing label option
prints the names and addresses of the members
selected. The meeting form letter prints ·a prepared
text advising the members of the next meeting. The
user supplies information such as time and place of
the meeting before the reports are generated. The
dues form letter prints a prepared text advising
the member that their dues payment is due
immediately. The text of both form letters is to be
easily alterable. Upon completion of each printout,
the program returns to the REPORTS sub-menu.

    The reports should be organized to fit on a
standard 8 1/2 x 11 inch fanfold sheet with tractor
feeds and should be clear and easy to read. Upon
entering the program, a top of form signal should
be sent to the line printer to begin printing on
the top of a new page.

ADDITIONAL SPECIFICATION

Now that the three programs (MENU, INPUT, and
REPORTS) have been defined, the master file
MEMBER/DAT should also be defined. The data that
must be contained in each file record has already
been determined. All that needs to be done now is
to detail this information in the program
specification.

Specification of MEMBER/DAT

    MEMBER/DAT is the master membership file that
is used by the program INPUT and REPORTS. All data

about each member is stored in this file. Each member is assigned one record in this file and all required data is placed in that record. The following convention is to be implemented:

Some characters will contain the name of the member using the convention last name, first name, with a space separating the two names.

Some characters will contain the number and street address of the member.

Some characters will contain the city, state, and zip code address of the member.

Some characters will contain the date of membership using the form MM-DD-YY or MM/DD/YY.

One character will contain a "Y" if yearly dues have been paid and an "N" if they have not been paid.

Some characters will contain the phone number of the member in the ###-###-#### format.

Each of these fields are alphanumeric because they could contain numbers or other symbols, such as letters or delimiters. The user will supply data, one field at a time, for a given member from program INPUT; with the option to erase the data and start again, or store the information in the fields as shown.

In our implementation of this file, the following convention will be used:

NAME - 30 characters for the last and first names, separated by a space

ADDRESS - 30 characters for number and street name, 20 characters for the city, state, and zip code

MEMBERSHIP DATE - 8 characters stored in the MM-DD-YY or MM/DD/YY convention

DUES STATUS - 1 character with a Y if paid and an N if not

PHONE NUMBER - 12 characters in ###-###-#### format

The total storage for one member is then 30 + 30 + 20 + 8 + 1 + 12 = 101 characters. This is therefore the record length of the file MEMBER/DAT.

In addition to the specification of MEMBER/DAT and the three programs, the final specification should include other factors. The amount of manpower allocated and the time limits which have been set are of great importance in a specification, since they play a role in evaluating the success of the project. The individuals assigned to take charge of the project should be listed and their responsibilities should be outlined. Periodic reviews of the project by

supervisors should be scheduled, whether they are
written reports or presentations. Finally, those
people with the authority to change the scope of
the final specification should be listed. Too often
individuals request changes after a progress review
that result in a substantial loss of time. If those
changes come from someone who is unaware of the
intent of those who require the program, conflict
may result. This slows down the program's
development while meetings and reviews begin to try
and resolve the situation. By delegating authority
to those with an interest in the program, the
programmers can be sure that suggestions and
changes are warranted and are done with the
knowledge of the other concerned parties.

This completes the specification of our sample
program. Each member of the committee should sign
the final document and receive a copy of it. All
decisions made by the programmers will come from
this specification. Each review of the development
is done according to the time intervals and
conditions set by the specification. Finally, the
acceptance or rejection of the finished program is
based upon the criteria set down in the
specification. With this task completed, the
programmer can now begin the task of designing and
implementing a solution.

REFERENCES

1. J. L. Elshoff, An Analysis of Some Commercial
    PL/I Programs, IEEE Transactions on Software
    Engineering, June 1976, pp. 113 - 120.

For additional information on PERT and CPM, consult:

Desmond D. Martin and Richard L. Shell,   What Every
    Engineer   Should   Know   About   Human   Resources
    Management   , Marcel Dekker Inc., 1980, pp. 50-54.

3

SOFTWARE DESIGN

This chapter will deal with the techniques used to
design computer programs. Using these techniques,
the programmer will convert the specification into
logic diagrams and flow charts. Later, these flow
charts will be implemented into actual computer
languages.

DETERMINATION OF RESOURCES

Before the programmer can begin to turn a
specification into a program, several decisions

must be   made. At this point the programmer   decides
what   resources are   required   to complete   the   job.
These   resources   include   manpower   requirements,
reference material,   and computer time.   Allocations
are   then   made   by   management for use   in   program
development.

Manpower   requirements   are   based   upon   the
number of software personnel needed to   complete the
job. Since   each   programmer may not   be working   on
one project   alone, the number of man-hours required
for   completion   of   the   program   could   also   be
specified.   A   team of individuals   is then selected
and the program is divided   among   them. Of   course,
some programs are so short that only   one individual
is responsible for the entire project.

Reference   material   may   also   be required   to
complete   the   program. Programmers   should   always
have information available that explains   the design
of   the   computer   they are using.   This   helps   the
programmer work around constraints   imposed   on   the
program   by   the   computer itself.   Since   computers
vary   widely   in characteristics such as   speed   and
memory,   a working   knowledge   of   each   machine   is
essential.   Reference   material   should   also   be
obtained   on   the   language   to   be   used.   Since
languages are not standardized to   any great extent,
the programmer   should determine   what   features are
included in   each   version   of available   languages.
Finally,   the   specification   of the program is   the
most important   reference   of   all.   If   it   is well

written and complete, most of the answers to
questions about design are found there.

Computer time requirements are estimates of
the amount of time needed to enter, debug, and save
the complete program. When a system is shared
between many users, sign-up sheets for use of the
facility is a common practice. Therefore, the
programmer needs to determine the amount of time
required. In addition, dates must be determined
when the programmer will finish the design phase
and begin to use the machine to enter the program.
In this way, the machine is free to be used by
others until it is required by the programmer, with
each programmer using the machine the least amount
of time possible.

Scheduling can be greatly enhanced through the
use of techniques such as CPM and PERT. An
explanation of these techniques is beyond the scope
of this book, but they are excellent ways to
determine the time needed to complete any project.
An explanation of these techniques is available in
most texts on management skills.

CHOOSING THE LANGUAGE

Once the programmer has determined and allocated
the resources needed, attention is focused on the

language choice, for which the following factors
should be considered:

Speed. As a general rule, high-level languages
are more removed from actual assembly
language and tend to take longer to execute
a given program. If the execution time is
critical or quick response is desired, a
language closer to assembly language must be
used. However, high-level languages
typically are easier to understand, more
powerful, and less complicated. A compromise
must be reached between complexity and speed
that will satisfy those concerns.

Application. Each language has unique strong
points and weaknesses. Some have excellent
graphical or computational capabilities.
Others are less structured and give the
programmer more freedom in the final program
design. Some offer broader or more powerful
instruction sets at the expense of memory or
speed. Again, a choice must be made that
matches a language with the application to
be implemented.

Portability. Often a program must be developed
to run on more than one computer. This can
be achieved by selecting a language offered
on several different machines. Many programs
available for today's microcomputers will
run on any machine which supports the CP/M
(TM Digital Research Corporation) operating

system. Thus, users can have different
computers and still manage to use the same
software.

Program Size. If the program is a large one,
then the choice of a language may be based
on other concerns. If many people wll be
involved in the programming process, a
language may be chosen that offers
flexiblity in letting each person write
parts of the program separately, linking
them in together after all modules have been
coded. This usually results in the use of a
language with a good compiler. A language
with strong type checking may also be
applicable, since maintenance can be more of
a problem in larger programs.

By considering these factors, the programmer
can select a language from the wide range
available. The programmer should then become
familiar with the instruction set of this language
and begin with some simple programs for experience.

DESIGN TECHNIQUES

There are many ways of applying the principle of
modular decomposition to a program. Recall that
this procedure subdivides the program by function
into smaller programs called modules. The two most
common techniques used, top/down and bottom/up,
will both be discussed here.

The top/down technique (also known as step-wise refinement) proceeds just as its name implies. The programmer begins with the organization of the mainline module and then proceeds to each module addressed by the mainline. These modules are then organized one at a time and the process is repeated with any sub-modules that must then be created to support modules on the next highest level. The process ends when all the modules have been defined. Figure 3.1 gives a pictorial representation of this procedure, showing how the programmer begins at the top level and works his way down to the bottom of the program.

In the bottom/up technique, the programmer begins by defining the lowest level modules first. Higher level modules are then written to link these lower level modules together. The process continues until the mainline program is written to link the entire program together. Figure 3.2 shows that this process is directly opposite of that shown in the top/down design representation.

Neither method has significant advantages over the other in terms of decomposition. The important point is that the program should be subdivided into smaller modules which are relatively independant of each other. This allows several programmers to begin coding the program so that their completed modules can be linked together without worrying about the contents of another module. This independance also allows the modules to be filed

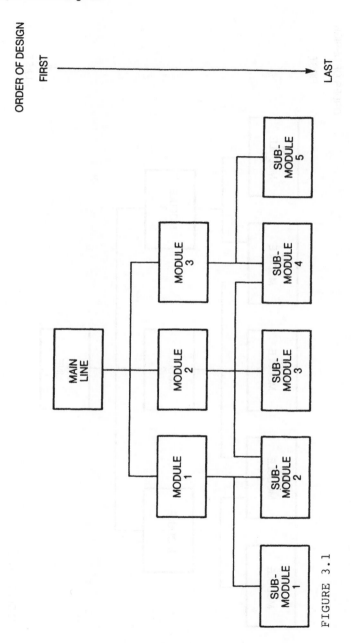

FIGURE 3.1

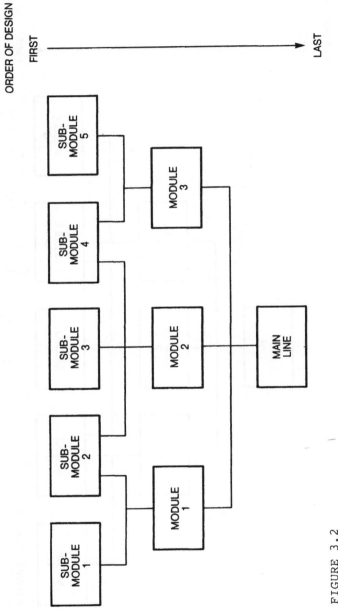

FIGURE 3.2

away in a software library and re-used when a
similar module is called for.

FLOW CHARTS

When the program has been decomposed into a
collection of modules, it is time to define what
each module should do. The operation performed by a
module is called an algorithm. An algorithm is a
finite number of steps that a computer performs to
complete a process and is composed of three parts.
One part of the algorithm is the processing phase,
in which mathematical calculations are performed
and data is processed. Another part is the test
phase, where a comparison is made between two items
and the result of this comparison is determined. In
essence, the computer decides what condition exists
after the comparison. The final part of an
algorithm is the branch phase. Based on a knowledge
of the result of a comparison, the computer may
continue the same process, terminate the program,
or jump to a new process. All that is required is
that an algorithm be developed that describes the
function to be implemented. The program can then be
generated by using any combination of these three
parts in the correct order.

Flow charts are the visual representation of
an algorithm. The programmer constructs flow charts
to better describe the procedure or function of a
particular module. Some of the basic symbols used
in flow charting are shown in Figure 3.3 . The
circle defines the start or finish of an algorithm,

and thus it appears at each end of a module. The rectangle indicates a procedure the computer follows which is usually described in brief detail inside the rectangle. The diamond is the symbol used to indicate a decision that is made by the machine. Arrows connect these symbols and indicate the direction of program flow.

A sample flow chart is shown in Figure 3.4 that computes the average of a list of numbers. The first process block shows the total and the number count are both zeroed. Next, a number is fetched and added to the total and the number counter is

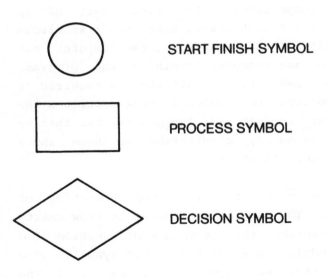

START FINISH SYMBOL

PROCESS SYMBOL

DECISION SYMBOL

FIGURE 3.3

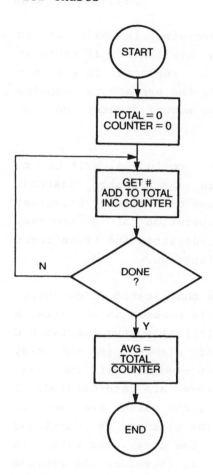

FIGURE 3.4

incremented by one. A decision is made as to
whether another number is available. If there is
another one, the process is repeated. If all the
numbers have been entered, the average is computed
by dividing the total by the number counter and the
average is obtained.

Note that a program could be written to
implement this function in any language desired.
Flow charts are therefore one of the most universal
ways of expressing the operation of a program,
since they can be easily understood and transferred
into a different computer language.

To illustrate a more complicated flow chart,
consider a program that sorts numbers in an array A
(as shown in Figure 3.5). Initially the variable C
is set to point to the first element in the array
and P points to the next element. If the next
element is smaller, the values are interchanged. If
the next element is larger, the values are kept in
their original positions. The process is continued
until P reaches the end of the array. The value in
position C of the array A is therefore the minimum
value of all the remaining elements in the array.
The value of C is then incremented to move to the
next position and the process is repeated until the
entire array is sorted from lowest to highest
values.

This example shows how a rather complicated
function can be segmented into a simple algorithm
through the use of flow charts. Note that the

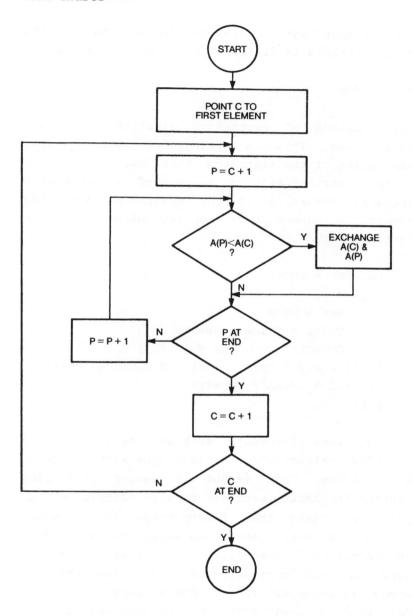

FIGURE 3.5

computer must make several decisions, the results
of which branch to different parts of the program.

PSUEDO CODE

Another method of expressing algorithms is with
psuedo code. This is nothing more than a verbal
description of the algorithm that may include some
of the instructions used as part of a computer´s
language. Returning to the example of averaging
numbers, a psuedo code representation of the
algorithm is:

```
COUNTER = TOTAL = 0
Repeat
    Get NUMBER
    TOTAL = TOTAL + NUMBER
    COUNTER = COUNTER + 1
Until every NUMBER is entered and none remain
AVERAGE = TOTAL / COUNTER
END.
```

Note that statements such as line 4 and line 5
are valid instructions in languages such as BASIC
and FORTRAN. This method is easier than flow
charting for larger programs because describing the
operations using the flowcharting method would
require far more pages than using the psuedo code
representation. However, for small, simple
algorithms with many decisions, the flow charting
method is superior. This is due in part to the fact
that process statements can be combined into a
single block, and program flow arrows will point to

the process, rather than directing the reader to a line number that stands for that process.

The sorting example would have a psuedo code representation of the algorithm that looks like this:

```
Point C to first element
Repeat
        Point P to element C + 1
        Repeat
            IF A(P) < A THEN exchange elements
            P = P + 1
        Until P points to end of the array + 1
        C = C + 1
Until C points to the end of the array
END.
```

This algorithm is identical to the one shown in Figure 3.5 and also includes some code-like statements as well as written explanations. Notice it is much easier to detect which loops are nested inside the others than with the flow chart with its flow arrows.

THE PROJECT WORKBOOK

Once development of the program design is complete, a project workbook should be constructed. This workbook should contain the following:

1. Program specification
2. Resource information which pertains to the program or the machine which it will run on

3. Resource information on the language chosen
4. Preliminary top / down or bottom / up design
   concepts
5. Flowchart of each module

As the program develops into working form, additional information such as program listings and documentation is added. In this way, another programmer can take over the project and changes can be made at a later date based on the documentation provided. This information can also serve as supporting evidence when decisions made about the program must be justified. At the end of the project the workbook will then be turned over to the software librarian, who will keep it on file so that anyone can have access to it.

THE DESIGN REVIEW

At this point, the design of the program has been accomplished. However, the program designed by the programmer may not be the one that those writing the specification had hoped for. To ensure that no further development time is spent on an unwanted or undesirable program, a design review is arranged. Members of the specification team sit down with the programmer and the chief programmer (see Chapter 1) and go over the flow charts or pseudo code representations together. While those who desire the program may not have a working knowledge of computer programs, explanations from the programmer will usually help them understand the algorithms involved. In this manner, conflicts can be resolved before the program is actually coded, which reduces the amount of effort spent on the project.

When an agreement is reached, the flow charts themselves become an integral part of the specification. The purpose and scope of the program is now clearly defined and it can be implemented in the language of the programmer´s choice. All that is required from this point on is the basic skills of computer programming: coding, testing, debugging, and documenting. The specification team no longer needs to supply input until a finished program is brought forward for their evaluation.

SUMMARY

Once the specification of a program is complete, the design process starts with the gathering of resources about both the machine and the selected language, scheduling of computer time, and determination of the manpower necessary to complete the project.

The program is then subdivided by modular decomposition into smaller sub-programs called modules. These modules are formed using either the top/down or bottom/up technique.

Once the modules have been defined, flow charts or pseudo codes are generated to describe the algorithm associated with that module. These flow charts are reviewed by the specification team to ensure they meet the specification´s requirements.

Finally, the specification, resource material, and flow charts are assembled into a project workbook. This workbook contains all applicable information on the program and will be updated continuously in succeeding steps in the structured program design process.

FLOW CHART EXAMPLES

The flow charts for the membership program discussed in Chapter 2 are now presented. Since this program is not a complex one, it is left to the reader to trace through the flow charts and understand what each module does. These modules will each be coded in Chapter 4 according to the flow charts shown. Note that some modules reference other modules and that these modules may in turn reference others. This process minimizes the amount of repetitive code and makes come of the modules general enough to be used over again.

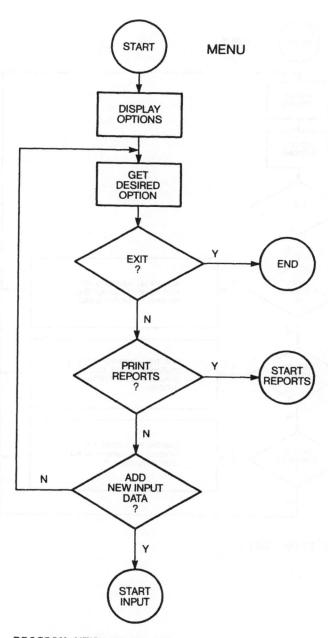

MENU

PROGRAM MENU FLOW CHART

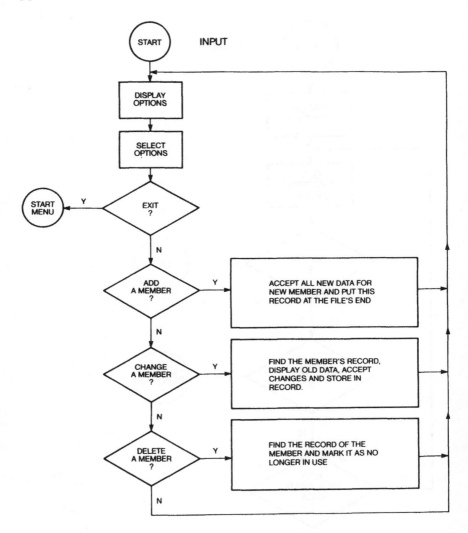

PROGRAM INPUT FLOW CHART

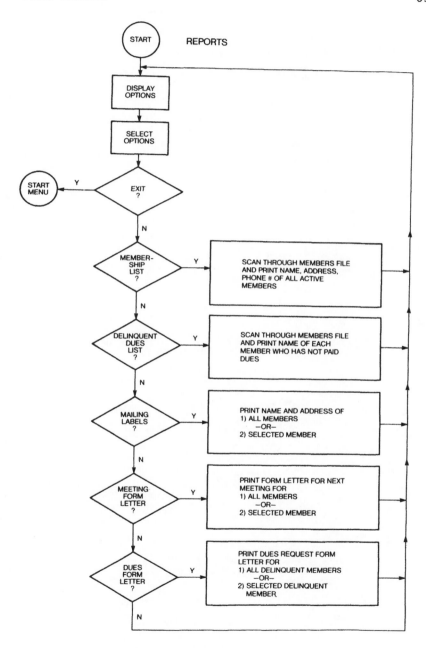

PROGRAM REPORTS FLOW CHART

4

CODING AND DEBUGGING SOFTWARE

This chapter focuses on the coding and debugging phases of the structured program design process. Up to this point, a specification has been written to outline the function of a desired program. This program has then been divided into small modules, each with its own independent function to perform. Each module is then detailed further by describing the function using an algorithm that is illustrated using flow charts or psuedo code. Finally, a main

67

line module is grouped with all the other function
modules to complete the program.

FLOW CHART CONVERSIONS TO PROGRAM CODE

The chief purpose of a flow chart or psuedo code
representation is to make an algorithm easy to
convert into computer instructions. Recall that an
algorithm is composed of three parts: processing,
testing and deciding, and branching upon decision.
The processing phase receives data and operates on
it in a specified manner. The test and decide phase
compares two or more pieces of data according to a
certain condition. The branch phase then jumps to
different parts of the program based upon the
result of the comparison. These three phases are
illustrated in flow charts through the use of
circles, rectangles, diamonds, and arrows to
indicate program flow.

    These three functions are included in every
computer language. Assembly language programmers
will find their instruction sets contain math
functions for processing, logical operations for
decision making, and a series of jump - on -
condition instructions that implement these
functions. Users of higher level languages such as
BASIC, FORTRAN, and PASCAL will find more advanced
math functions (such as multiplication and
division) and decision and branch instructions
combined into statements such as IF...THEN...ELSE.
Nearly all other languages provide processing
functions such as the arithmetic group of addition,

subtraction,   multiplication,   and   division.
Decisions   are   generated   using   the   logical
operations and tests of less than, equal to, or
greater than zero. Some include branches upon error
conditions such as overflow and underflow. A wide
range of other instructions also exist and the
programmer is advised to become familiar with the
specific languages to utilize these instructions.

    Since   there   are   comparable instructions for
the flow chart symbols that have been defined, flow
charts can be directly converted to program code
simply by using the equivalent program instruction
for the desired steps. By using this matching
technique, programs written in computer code will
mirror the flow charts that described them. This
makes the job of detecting errors much easier,
since program errors will correspond to those in
the flow chart.

TYPES OF DOCUMENTATION

Documentation is the information provided by the
programmer to explain the operation of a program.
This area is often overlooked but is vitally
important when modifications must be made. Several
types of documentation can be provided, and
programmers should prepare as much documentation as
required to completely specify a program.

    Because of their "mirror effect" with the
program itself, flow charts are an excellent source
of documentation. A newcomer to the program can

easily   relate   to   it   by   following   the   simple
symbols, and it requires   no prior knowledge   of the
language that was used.

Another   type of   documentation   is implemented
when   comments are   placed   in   the   program itself.
When a program includes   comments,   it is known as a
self-documented   program. Programs   of   this   type
usually   have   comments   every   second   or   third
statement   that describe   what those statements   do.
These   comments   could   be   a   psuedo-code
representation of the program or short   explanations
of   the   functions   performed.   This   type   of
self-documenting code also eliminates   the   need for
completely   understanding   the language   used, since
the algorithm   is   outlined as it   is implemented in
the   computer   program.   This   method   is   usually
preferred over others because   the documentation   is
part   of   the   program and   cannot be   misplaced   or
lost.   It also   forms   a direct relationship between
the algorithm   and the sequence of instructions that
implement it.

In   addition to   the self-documenting   comments
that   can   be contained   in   a program,   it is often
useful to include brief   comments   at   the start   of
each   module   that   describe   its   function.   This
technique is known as   HIPO,   or   Hierarchial   Input
Process   Output   documentation.   This   type   of
documentation   views the   module   as   a   "black   box"
with   certain   characteristics. Inputs   representing
some   type of data are   fed   into   the module, which
then processes them in   some   described manner.   The

results of this processing are then fed out of the module to be used as data for another module.

Inputs and outputs of a module are known as parameters. We can then speak of inputs as parameters which are "passed in" to the module and outputs which are "passed out" from the module. Parameter passing is a popular way of taking a general module and having it perform a specific function determined by the input parameters passed to it. For example, a module which prints letters on a display screen could have the letters to be printed, and how many letters should be printed, as input parameters.

A HIPO documentation block describes a module in terms of these three characteristics. First, the process contained in the module is briefly described so that others can understand the programmer´s intent. Next, the input parameters are listed and defined as to how they affect the performance of the module. Finally, the output parameters are specified and described so the results of the process can be used as input for another module. A well-structured program should then have a mainline program which sets up the first set of parameters, calls the first module, and uses the output of that module with other new parameters to call a second module, and so forth. HIPO documentation allows the programmer to describe each module to someone else without requiring them to understand the algorithm used to implement the solution. The advantages of this type

of documentation will be   shown in later sections of
this chapter. Examples of HIPO documenation are
included at the end of this chapter.

   By using a combination of HIPO documentation
and self - documenting program code, the programmer
can describe the program clearly and concisely.   The
HIPO block provides a brief description of the
intent of the programmer and the self - documenting
code provides additional information about the
algorithm used and its implementation. These two
techniques should be used together to supply all
necessary information about the program to those
who will use or modify it once it is released.

THE STRUCTURED WALK-THROUGH

Once the program has been transferred from flow
charts into a computer language, the debugging
process begins. The first step in error detection
should be the structured walk-through. The
programmer enters the program into the computer and
corrects any minor syntax errors before the
walk-through begins. He then presents his listings
to the programming staff for review. This step
helps catch most of the major errors in programming
before the program is even executed on the machine
and tested.

   The structured .walk-through is a meeting of
the programming staff that reviews the operation of
a program to find errors and make suggestions about
ways to improve the program. The meeting is usually

called at the request of the programmer and the
chief programmer. Since this is a technical review
or comparison to the specification, members of
management need not be present. The purpose of this
meeting is for other programmers to review the work
done to date and use the documentation provided.
This ensures that correct algorithms are used and
that they are implemented properly. The programmer
is available to answer questions about the design
process but should not "sell" the implementation of
the program. This allows others to view the work
from an objective viewpoint and make
recommendations based on interpretations and
experience.

In addition to the comments made, several
programmers can also emulate the computer by
pretending to "execute" the program themselves and
look for errors. In this way, the programmers can
determine how the machine will interpret the
program and verify that this interpretation will
achieve the required results. Errors can then be
found and corrected before the program is ever put
into a machine.

Although the walk-through process may seem
wasteful because of the number of people involved,
the resulting savings in debugging time more than
outweigh the review time. Organizations with
continual software development should consider
structured walk-throughs as an integral part of the
periodic design reviews. Since most organizations
never hesitate to review hardware designs before

their release, equal consideration should be given
to peer review of software projects. In addition,
the structured walk-through is an excellent way for
programmers to see other methods of implementing a
solution. This allows each programmer to help
disseminate their programming skills in a
particular area to others, improving the skills of
every other programmer.

DEBUGGING IN THE COMPUTER

When the structured walk-through has been
completed, the program is ready to be tested in the
computer. Several hints will be useful in speeding
up the troubleshooting process.

   One of the easiest ways to troubleshoot
software is on a module-by-module basis. Just as
subdividing made the process of design easier,
modular debugging simplifies the troubleshooting
process. The programmer should begin by writing
short programs that configure a set of input
parameters, call the module to be tested, and then
inform the programmer of the results. The
programmer can then evaluate the results and
determine if the module is functioning correctly.
Testing each module on an individual basis such as
this minimizes the amount of a program tested at
one time. This approach allows the programmer to
concentrate on individual areas without having to
be concerned about the entire system.

The programmer can also add statements to the modules that will inform him how the computer progresses through the module. Statements which print brief descriptions at the end of loops or after decisions have been made by the machine help in determining how the machine interprets the sequence of instructions. These extra statements can then be removed at the end of the debugging phase, leaving the program intact.

Another useful tool for the debugging process is a development system. Some computers have software features such as break points, memory dumps, program traces, and others that allow the programmer to analyze the steps the computer took in executing the program. Development systems are an excellent investment for firms that are constantly involved in the software design process and want to improve efficiency.

Finally, the greatest asset in debugging a program is the actual programmer. Since the author of a particular piece of software knows it better than anyone, that person should be consulted when errors are found. Sound reasoning, logical thinking, and a few reference books are helpful tools for the programmer in debugging. Moreover, patience and perseverance can overcome frustration and anxiety, so that most bugs become nothing more than trivial mistakes.

SUMMARY

The entire debugging process can be described with
the simple phrase, "fix it, file it, forget it."
This procedure encompasses the entire process of
documentation and troubleshooting into three steps.

     The "fix it" step pertains to the removal of
program errors, or "bugs." Using all the resources
gathered to date (such as flow charts and reference
material) the programmer corrects the code until it
performs the desired function and documents it. The
programmer debugs the program on a module-by-module
basis until the entire program is done.

     When the debugging phase is over, the
programmer turns over a copy of his modules and
documentation to the software librarian. Other
programmers can then use these modules and a copy
is made to guard against the program somehow being
destroyed. This library of programs is a valuable
resource when new programs are written and can
provide another source of ideas.

     When the program has been debugged and filed,
the algorithms are essentially forgotten by the
author. Since there is plenty of documentation, the
programmer should have no trouble resuming the
project at a later date. Those interested in
specific modules need not scan the entire code but
can get a brief description from the HIPO comment
block at the start of each module. A closer
examination can be made of the modules which are of

interest   based   upon   the   HIPO   information.
Modifications can then be made on a copy of a
module to suit other   purposes.   This new module can
the be   re-filed   with   additional documentation. In
this way, the   software library has   information on
all programs and modifications available.

SAMPLE PROGRAM

The   program   listings   for   the   programs   MENU,
REPORTS, and INPUT appear in the next few pages.
Note that special routines   such   as the display I/O
and file manipulation appear in more than one of
the programs. These programs are   written   in BASIC
developed by MicroSoft, and are compatible with a
great   range   of   machines   with only   a   few
modifications.   The   apostrophe is used in this
language to denote a comment field and   comments are
provided   using   the   self   -   documenting and   HIPO
methods.

```
1  'PROGRAM MENU
2  'COPYRIGHT 1984 - KEITH R. WEHMEYER
3  'THIS PROGRAM IS THE MAIN MENU FOR OUR EXAMPLE MEMBERSHIP
4  'PROGRAM. WHEN YOU RUN THIS PROGRAM, YOU HAVE 3 CHOICES:
5  '
6  '        1 - JUMP TO THE INPUT PROGRAM
7  '        2 - JUMP TO THE REPORTS PROGRAM
8  '        3 - EXIT THE PROGRAM AND RETURN TO THE OPERATING SYSTEM
9  'THE INPUT PROGRAM UPDATES MEMBERSHIP DATA AND THE REPORTS
10 'PROGRAM PRINTS VARIOUS FORM LETTERS AND LISTS ON A
11 'HARDCOPY DEVICE, SUCH AS A LINE PRINTER.
12 '
20 CLS
25 PRINT` 19,"EXAMPLE MEMBERSHIP PROGRAM"
30 PRINT` 152,"OPTIONS AVAILABLE:"
35 PRINT` 200,"1 - MEMBER MANAGEMENT         2 - REPORT PRINTOUT"
40 PRINT`332,"ADD MEMBERS":PRINT`360,"MEMBERSHIP LIST"
45 PRINT`396,"CHANGE MEMBER":PRINT`424,"DUES LIST"
50 PRINT`460,"DELETE MEMBER":PRINT`488,"MAILING LABELS"
55 PRINT`552,"MEETING LETTER"
60 PRINT`616,"DUES LETTER"
65 PRINT`732,"3 - EXIT"
70 T$ = "ENTER MENU OPTION (1-3) ":UL=3:LL=1:GOSUB 5005
75 IF K = 1 THEN RUN "INPUT/BAS"
80 IF K = 2 THEN RUN "REPORTS/BAS"
85 IF K = 3 THEN CMD "S" 'EXIT TO OPERATING SYSTEM
90 STOP
5000 'CONSOLE DATA FETCH ROUTINE
5001 'PRINTS TEXT STRING, PROMPTS FOR AN INPUT, AND CHECKS
5002 'TO SEE THAT THE VALUE LIES BETWEEN THE UPPER AND LOWER
5003 'LIMITS. IF IT DOES NOT, THE USER IS RE-PROMPTED TO
5004 'TRY AGAIN. RETURNS WITH THE SELECTION IN VARIABLE K.
5005 PRINT`896,CHR$(31) 'ERASES TO END OF SCREEN
5010 PRINT`896,T$;
5015 INPUT K
5020 IF K < LL THEN 5035
5025 IF K > UL THEN 5035
5030 RETURN
5035 PRINT`960,"INCORRECT RESPONSE";
5040 FOR K = 1 TO 1000:NEXT K:GOTO 5005
9999 END
```

PROGRAM MENU

```
1  'PROGRAM INPUT
2  'COPYRIGHT 1984 - KEITH R. WEHMEYER
3  'THIS PROGRAM MODIFIES THE MEMBERSHIP RECORDS IN THE FILE
4  'MEMBER/DAT. WHEN YOU RUN THE PROGRAM, YOU HAVE 4 CHOICES:
5  '        1 - ADD A MEMBERSHIP RECORD
6  '        2 - CHANGE A MEMBERSHIP RECORD
7  '        3 - DELETE A MEMBERSHIP RECORD
8  '        4 - EXIT BACK TO THE MENU PROGRAM.
10 CLEAR 2000
20 CLS
25 PRINT`18,"MEMBERSHIP RECORDS PROCESSING"
30 PRINT`152,"OPTIONS AVAILABLE:"
35 PRINT`216,"1 - ADD A MEMBER"
40 PRINT`280,"2 - CHANGE A MEMBER"
45 PRINT`344,"3 - DELETE A MEMBER"
50 PRINT`472,"4 - EXIT TO MAIN MENU"
55 T$="ENTER PROCESSING OPTION (1-4) ":UL=4:LL=1:GOSUB 5005
60 CLS
65 IF K = 1 THEN 500 'ADD MEMBER ROUTINE
70 IF K = 2 THEN 1000 'CHANGE MEMBER ROUTINE
75 IF K = 3 THEN 1500 'DELETE MEMBER ROUTINE
80 RUN "MENU/BAS" 'EXIT TO MAIN MENU
490 'ADD MEMBER OPTION
491 'ALLOWS USER TO INPUT ALL MEMBER DATA THROUGH AN
492 'INTERACTIVE PROCESS AND SAVE IN THE FILE MEMBER/DAT
493 'OR RESTART OR EXIT THE OPTION TO THE INPUT MENU
500 OPEN "R",1,"MEMBER/DAT":FIELD 1,101 AS F1$
505 R = LOF(1)+1
510 N$ = STRING$(30," ") 'INITIALIZE NAME STRING
515 A$ = STRING$(30," ") 'INITIALIZE ADDRESS STRING
520 C$ = STRING$(20," ") 'INITIALIZE CITY,STATE,ZIP STRING
525 D$ = STRING$(8," ")  'INITIALIZE DUES STATUS
530 S$ = STRING$(1," ")  'INTIALIZE DUES STATUS
535 P$ = STRING$(12," ") 'INTIALIZE PHONE NUMBER STRING
540 CLS
545 PRINT`27,"ADD MEMBER"
548 'PRINT THE FIELDS OF INFORMATION LISTINGS AND PRINT
549 'THE ENTERED DATA FOR EACH FIELD AFTER THE PROMPT
550 GOSUB 3000
555 T$ = "ENTER NAME (1-30 CHAR.) ":GOSUB 6000
560 N$ = MID$(K$,1,30):GOSUB 3500
565 T$ = "ENTER ADDRESS ":GOSUB 6000
570 A$ = MID$(K$,1,30):GOSUB 3500
575 T$ = "ENTER CITY STATE AND ZIP ":GOSUB 6000
580 C$ = MID$(K$,1,20):GOSUB 3500
585 T$ = "ENTER DATE (MM-DD-YY) ":GOSUB 6000
590 D$ = MID$(K$,1,8):GOSUB 3500
595 T$ = "ENTER DUES STATUS (Y OR N) ":GOSUB 6000
600 S$ = "N"
605 IF MID$(K$,1,1) = "Y" THEN S$ = "Y" 'OTHERWISE NOT PAID
610 GOSUB 3500
615 T$ = "ENTER PHONE NUMBER (###-###-####) ":GOSUB 6000
620 P$ = MID$(K$,1,12):GOSUB 3500
625 T$ = "ENTER 1 TO SAVE, 2 TO START OVER, OR 3 TO QUIT"
630 LL=1:UL=3:GOSUB 5000
635 IF K = 2 THEN 510
640 IF K = 3 THEN 650
645 GOSUB 4000 'SAVE ADDITIONS IN MEMBER/DAT
650 PRINT "DATA SAVED IN RECORD ";
655 PRINT R
660 CLOSE 1:GOTO 20
```

PROGRAM INPUT

```
990  'CHANGE MEMBER OPTION
991  'ALLOWS USER TO CHANGE ALL MEMBER DATA THROUGH AN
992  'INTERACTIVE PROCESS AND SAVE IN THE FILE MEMBER/DAT
993  'OR RESTART OR EXIT BACK TO THE INPUT MENU
1000 OPEN "R",1,"MEMBER/DAT"
1005 CLS:PRINT`28,"CHANGE MEMBER"
1010 T$ = "ENTER MEMBER NUMBER (RETURN TO EXIT) ":GOSUB 6000
1015 IF K$ = STRING$(64," ") THEN 1155
1020 R = VAL(K$)
1025 IF (R < 1) OR (R > LOF(1)) THEN 1005
1030 FIELD 1,101 AS F1$
1035 GET 1,R
1040 N$ = MID$(F1$,1,30)
1045 A$ = MID$(F1$,31,30)
1050 C$ = MID$(F1$,61,20)
1055 D$ = MID$(F1$,81,8)
1060 S$ = MID$(F1$,89,1)
1065 P$ = MID$(F1$,90,12)
1070 GOSUB 3000:GOSUB 3500 'RECORD IS FETCHED SO PRINT IT
1075 T$ = "ENTER NAME CHANGE ":GOSUB 6000
1080 IF K$ <> STRING$(64," ") THEN LSET N$ = MID$(K$,1,30):GOSUB 3500
1085 T$ = "ENTER ADDRESS CHANGE ":GOSUB 6000
1090 IF K$ <> STRING$(64," ") THEN LSET A$ = MID$(K$,1,30):GOSUB 3500
1095 T$ = "ENTER CITY STATE ZIP CHANGE ":GOSUB 6000
1100 IF K$ <> STRING$(64," ") THEN LSET C$ = MID$(K$,1,20):GOSUB 3500
1105 T$ = "ENTER MEMBERSHIP DATE CHANGE ":GOSUB 6000
1110 IF K$ <> STRING$(64," ") THEN LSET D$ = MID$(K$,1,8):GOSUB 3500
1115 T$ = "ENTER DUES STATUS CHANGE ":GOSUB 6000
1120 IF K$ = STRING$(64," ") THEN 1125
1121 IF MID$(K$,1,1) = "Y" THEN S$ = "Y" ELSE S$ = "N"
1122 GOSUB 3500
1125 T$ = "ENTER PHONE CHANGE ":GOSUB 6000
1130 IF K$ <> STRING$(64," ") THEN LSET P$ = MID$(K$,1,12):GOSUB 3500
1135 T$ = "DO YOU WISH TO CANCEL AND RESTART (Y OR N) ":GOSUB 6000
1140 IF MID$(K$,1,1) = "Y" THEN 1005
1145 GOSUB 4000 'STORE AWAY CHANGES INTO MEMBER/DAT
1150 GOTO 1005
1155 CLOSE 1:GOTO 20 'END OF CHANGE MEMBER
1497 'DELETE MEMBER OPTION
1498 'DELETES RECORD FROM MEMBER/DAT, COMPRESSES THE FILE
1499 'INTO A TEMP FILE, AND RETURNS IT TO MEMBER/DAT
1500 CLS:PRINT`(27),"DELETE MEMBER"
1505 OPEN "R",1,"MEMBER/DAT":FIELD 1,101 AS F1$
1510 T$ = "ENTER MEMBER NUMBER (RETURN TO EXIT) ":GOSUB 6000
1515 IF K$ = STRING$(64," ") THEN 1635 'EXIT COMMAND OPTION
1520 R = VAL(K$) 'GET MEMBER NUMBER
1525 IF (R < 1) OR (R > LOF(1)) THEN 1510 'ILLEGAL NUMBER
1530 GET 1,R 'GET THAT RECORD TO BE DELETED
1535 PRINT`325, "RECORDS OF ",MID$(F1$,1,30);
1540 T$ = "DELETE ":GOSUB 6000
1550 IF K$ <> "Y" THEN 1510
1555 OPEN "R",2,"TEMP/DAT":FIELD 2,101 AS F2$
1560 IF R = 1 THEN 1580
1565 C = 1
1570 GET 1,C:LSET F2$ = F1$:PUT 2,C:C = C + 1
1575 IF C <> R THEN 1570 'REPEAT TRANSFER FOR ALL IN FRONT OF R
1580 IF R = LOF(1) THEN 1600
1585 C = R + 1 'SKIP OVER RECORD R
1590 GET 1,C:LSET F2$ = F1$:PUT 2,C:C = C + 1
1595 IF C <> LOF(1) + 1 THEN 1590 'STORE ALL REMAINING RECORDS
1600 CLOSE 1:KILL "MEMBER/DAT" 'REMOVE OLD FILE
1605 OPEN "R",1,"MEMBER/DAT":FIELD 1,101 AS F1$ 'START NEW ONE
1607 IF LOF(2) = 0 THEN 1625
1610 C = 1
1615 GET 2,C:LSET F1$ = F2$:PUT 1,C:C = C + 1
1620 IF C <> LOF(2) + 1 THEN 1615
```

PROGRAM INPUT (continued)

```
1625 CLOSE 2:KILL "TEMP/DAT" ´ALL DONE, FILE TRANSFERED
1630 GOTO 1510
1635 CLOSE 1: GOTO 20 ´EXIT DELETE MEMBER ROUTINE
2997 ´SUBROUTINE TO PRINT THE CATEGORIES STORED IN THE
2998 ´MEMBER/DAT FILE
3000 PRINT`133,"NAME"
3005 PRINT`197,"ADDRESS"
3010 PRINT@261,"CITY STATE ZIP"
3015 PRINT@325,"MEMBERSHIP DATE"
3020 PRINT@389,"DUES STATUS"
3025 PRINT@453,"PHONE NUMBER"
3030 RETURN
3498 ´SUBROUTINE TO PRINT OUT THE VALUES FOR EACH FIELD IN
3499 ´A PARTICULAR MEMBER RECORD OF MEMBER/DAT FILE
3500 PRINT@153,N$;  ´PRINT NAME
3505 PRINT@217,A$;  ´PRINT ADDRESS
3510 PRINT@281,C$;  ´PRINT CITY STATE ZIP
3515 PRINT`345,D$;  ´PRINT MEMBERSHIP DATE
3520 PRINT@409,S$;  ´PRINT DUES STATUS
3525 PRINT@473,P$;  ´PRINT PHONE NUMBER
3530 RETURN
3997 ´SUBROUTINE TO STORE NEW STRINGS INTO A RECORD OF A
3998 ´MEMBERS FILE. THE NAME, ADDRESS, CITY, MEMBERSHIP DATE
3999 ´DUES STATUS, AND PHONE NUMBER ARE STORED IN RECORD R
4000 V$ = STRING$(101," "):MID$(V$,1,30) = N$ ´SAVE NAME FIELD
4005 MID$(V$,31,30) = A$ ´SAVE ADDRESS
4010 MID$(V$,61,20) = C$ ´SAVE CITY, STATE, ZIP
4015 MID$(V$,81,8) = D$ ´SAVE MEMBERSHIP DATE
4020 MID$(V$,89,1) = S$ ´SAVE DUES STATUS
4025 MID$(V$,90,12) = P$ ´SAVE PHONE NUMBER
4030 LSET F1$ = V$
4035 PUT 1,R
4040 RETURN
5000 ´CONSOLE DATA FETCH ROUTINE
5001 ´PRINTS TEXT STRING, PROMPTS FOR AN INPUT, AND CHECKS
5002 ´TO SEE THAT THE VALUE LIES BETWEEN THE UPPER AND LOWER
5003 ´LIMITS. IF IT DOES NOT, THE USER IS RE-PROMPTED TO
5004 ´TRY AGAIN. RETURNS WITH THE SELECTION IN VARIABLE K.
5005 PRINT`896,CHR$(31) ´ERASE TO END OF SCREEN
5010 PRINT`896,T$;
5015 INPUT K
5020 IF K < LL THEN 5035
5025 IF K > UL THEN 5035
5030 RETURN
5035 PRINT`960,"INCORRECT RESPONSE";
5040 FOR K = 1 TO 1000:NEXT K:GOTO 5005
5998 ´SUBROUTINE TO FETCH A STRING RATHER THAN A NUMBER
5999 ´OPERATES LIKE SUBROUTINE LOCATED AT LINE 5000
6000 PRINT`896,CHR$(31)
6005 K$ = STRING$(64," ")
6010 PRINT`896,T$;
6015 INPUT K$
6020 RETURN
```

PROGRAM INPUT (continued)

```
1  'PROGRAM REPORTS
2  'COPYRIGHT 1984 - KEITH R. WEHMEYER
3  'THIS PROGRAM PRINTS OUT VARIOUS LISTS AND LETTERS
4  'USING THE MEMBERSHIP DATA FILE MEMBER/DAT.
5  'WHEN YOU RUN THIS PROGRAM, YOU HAVE 6 OPTIONS:
6  '        1 - MEMBERSHIP LIST PRINTOUT
7  '        2 - DUES PAYMENT LIST
8  '        3 - MAILING LABEL LIST
9  '        4 - MEETING ANNOUNCEMENT LETTER
10 '        5 - DELINQUENT DUES LETTER
11 '        6 - EXIT BACK TO MENU PROGRAM
20 CLS
25 PRINT`20,"REPORT PRINTOUT PROGRAM"
30 PRINT`152,"OPTIONS AVAILABLE"
35 PRINT`214,"1 - MEMBERSHIP LIST PRINTOUT"
40 PRINT`278,"2 - DELINQUENT DUES LIST"
45 PRINT`342,"3 - MAILING LABEL PRINTOUT"
50 PRINT`406,"4 - MEETING ANNOUNCEMENT LETTER"
55 PRINT`470,"5 - DELINQUENT DUES LETTER"
60 PRINT`598,"6 - EXIT TO MAIN MENU"
65 T$ = "ENTER PRINTOUT OPTION (1-6)":LL=1:UL=6:GOSUB 5005
70 CLS
75 IF K=1 THEN 500 'MEMBERSHIP LIST
80 IF K=2 THEN 1000 'DELINQUENT DUES LIST
85 IF K=3 THEN 1500 'MAILING LABEL LIST
90 IF K=4 THEN 2000 'MEETING ANNOUNCEMENT
95 IF K=5 THEN 2500 'DELINQUENT DUES LETTER
100 RUN "MENU/BAS" 'EXIT TO MAIN MENU
490 'MEMBERSHIP LIST PRINTOUT
500 CLS:PRINT`24,"MEMBERSHIP LIST"
505 OPEN "R",1,"MEMBER/DAT":FIELD 1,101 AS F1$
510 IF LOF(1) <> 0 THEN 525
515 CLS:PRINT`27,"NO MEMBERS":FOR I = 1 TO 1000:NEXT I
520 GOTO 595
525 R = 1 'POINT TO FIRST RECORD
527 LPRINT CHR$(11): PRINT "HIT ENTER WHEN READY":INPUT K$
528 GOTO 531
530 LPRINT CHR$(11)
531 LPRINT TAB(32) "MEMBERSHIP LIST":LPRINT
535 C = 1 'SET PAGE COUNTER TO ONE
540 GET 1,R : GOSUB 4000
545 LPRINT TAB(5) "RECORD NUMBER ",R
550 LPRINT TAB(5) N$
555 LPRINT TAB(5) A$ 'PRINT ADDRESS
560 LPRINT TAB(5) C$ 'PRINT CITY, STATE, ZIP CODE
565 LPRINT TAB(5) P$ 'PRINT PHONE NUMBER
570 LPRINT TAB(5) "MEMBERSHIP DATE ",D$
575 LPRINT:LPRINT
580 R = R + 1: C = C + 1 'INCREMENT BOTH COUNTERS
585 IF R = LOF(1) + 1 THEN 595 'EXIT IF DONE '
590 IF C < 8 THEN 540 ELSE 530 'NEW PAGE EVERY 8 ENTRIES
595 CLOSE 1: GOTO 20 'END OF MEMBERSHIP LIST PRINTOUT
990 'DELINQUENT DUES LIST
1000 CLS:PRINT`21,"DELINQUENT DUES LIST"
1005 OPEN "R",1,"MEMBER/DAT":FIELD 1,101 AS F1$
1010 IF LOF(1) <> 0 THEN 1025
1015 CLS: PRINT`27,"NO MEMBERS":FOR I = 1 TO 1000: NEXT I
1020 GOTO 1075
1025 R = 1 'POINT TO FIRST RECORD
1026 LPRINT CHR$(11):PRINT "HIT ENTER WHEN READY":INPUT K$
1027 GOTO 1031
1030 LPRINT CHR$(11)
1031 LPRINT TAB(30) "DELINQUENT DUES LIST":LPRINT
```

PROGRAM REPORTS

```
1035 C = 1 ´SET PAGE COUNTER TO ONE
1040 GET 1,R:GOSUB 4000 ´GET THE RECORD
1045 IF S$ = "Y" THEN 1055
1050 LPRINT TAB(5) N$:C = C + 1:LPRINT ´PRINT NAME IF DUE
1055 R = R + 1 ´ON TO NEXT MEMBER
1060 IF R = LOF(1) + 1 THEN 1075 ´ EXIT IF DONE
1065 IF C < 29 THEN 1040 ´29 MEMBER NAMES PER PAGE
1070 GOTO 1030
1075 CLOSE 1: GOTO 20
1490 ´ MAILING LABEL PRINTOUT
1500 CLS:PRINT`25,"MAILING LABELS"
1505 OPEN "R",1,"MEMBER/DAT":FIELD 1,101 AS F1$
1510 IF LOF(1) <> 0 THEN 1525
1515 CLS:PRINT`27,"NO MEMBERS":FOR I = 1 TO 1000:NEXT I
1520 GOTO 1585
1525 R = 1 ´POINT TO FIRST RECORD
1526 LPRINT CHR$(11):PRINT"HIT ENTER WHEN READY":INPUT K$
1527 LPRINT:GOTO 1535
1530 LPRINT CHR$(11):LPRINT
1535 C = 1 ´SET PAGE COUNTER TO ONE
1540 GET 1,R:GOSUB 4000
1545 LPRINT TAB(20) N$ ´PRINT NAME
1550 LPRINT TAB(20) A$ ´PRINT ADDRESS
1555 LPRINT TAB(20) C$ ´PRINT CITY, STATE, ZIP CODE
1560 LPRINT:LPRINT
1565 R = R + 1:C = C + 1 ´INCREMENT BOTH COUNTERS
1570 IF R = LOF(1) + 1 THEN 1585
1575 IF C < 12 THEN 1540 ´11 LABELS PER PAGE
1580 GOTO 1530
1585 CLOSE 1:GOTO 20
1990 ´MEETING ANNOUNCEMENT FORM LETTER
2000 CLS:PRINT`18,"MEETING ANNOUNCEMENT LETTER"
2005 T$ = "ENTER THE MEETING´S LOCATION ":GOSUB 6000
2010 L$ = K$ ´GET LOCATION
2015 T$ = "ENTER THE DATE OF THE MEETING ":GOSUB 6000
2020 D$ = K$
2025 T$ = "ENTER THE TIME OF THE MEETING ":GOSUB 6000
2030 TI$ = K$
2035 T$ = "ENTER THE MAIN ITEM OF BUSINESS ":GOSUB 6000
2040 B$ = K$
2045 T$ = "HOW MANY COPIES ":GOSUB 6000
2050 C = VAL(K$)
2055 LPRINT CHR$(11)
2060 FOR I = 1 TO C
2065 LPRINT TAB(5)"DEAR MEMBER,":LPRINT
2070 LPRINT TAB(10)"OUR NEXT MEETING WILL BE HELD ON ",D$:LPRINT
2075 LPRINT TAB(5)"AT ",TI$,". WE WILL MEET AT ",L$,"."
2080 LPRINT TAB(5)"OUR MAIN TOPIC OF DISCUSSION WILL BE ",B$,".":LPRINT
2085 LPRINT TAB(5)"HOPE TO SEE YOU THERE!"
2087 LPRINT CHR$(11)
2090 NEXT I
2095 GOTO 20
2499 ´DELINQUENT DUES LETTER
2500 CLS:PRINT`18,"DELINQUENT DUES LETTER"
2505 T$ = "HOW MANY COPIES ":GOSUB 6000
2510 C = VAL(K$)
2515 IF C = 0 THEN 20
2520 LPRINT CHR$(11) ´TOP IF FORM
2525 FOR I = 1 TO C
2530 LPRINT TAB(5)"DEAR MEMBER, ":LPRINT
2535 LPRINT TAB(10)"OUR RECORDS INDICATE THAT YOU HAVE NOT YET PAID YOUR DUES."
2540 LPRINT TAB(15)"PLEASE SEND US YOUR PAYMENT IMMEDIATELY OR BRING IT TO"
2545 LPRINT TAB(10)"THE NEXT MEETING. IF YOU HAVE ALREADY SENT IN YOUR"
2550 LPRINT TAB(10)"PAYMENT, PLEASE DISREGARD THIS NOTICE."
2552 LPRINT CHR$(11)
2555 NEXT I
```

PROGRAM REPORTS (continued)

```
2560 GOTO 20
3990 'SUBROUTINE TO GET ONE RECORD FROM THE MASTER MEMBERSHIP
3991 'FILE. RETURNED IN VARIOUS STRINGS.
4000 N$ = MID$(F1$,1,30)
4005 A$ = MID$(F1$,31,30)
4010 C$ = MID$(F1$,61,20)
4015 D$ = MID$(F1$,81,8)
4020 S$ = MID$(F1$,89,1)
4025 P$ = MID$(F1$,90,12)
4030 RETURN
5000 'CONSOLE DATA FETCH ROUTINE
5001 'PRINTS TEXT STRING, PROMPTS FOR AN INPUT, AND CHECKS
5002 'TO SEE THAT THE VALUE LIES BETWEEN THE UPPER AND LOWER
5003 'LIMITS. IF IT DOES NOT, THE USER IS RE-PROMPTED TO
5004 'TRY AGAIN. RETURNS WITH THE SELECTION IN VARIABLE K.
5005 PRINT`896,CHR$(31)
5010 PRINT`896,T$;
5015 INPUT K
5020 IF K < LL THEN 5035
5025 IF K > UL THEN 5035
5030 RETURN
5035 PRINT "INCORRECT RESPONSE";
5040 FOR K=1 TO 1000:NEXT K:GOTO 5005
5999 'CONSOLE FETCH ROUTINE FOR ALPHANUMERIC CHARACTERS
6000 K$ = STRINGS$(64," ")
6005 PRINT@896, CHR$(31)
6010 PRINT`896, T$
6015 INPUT K$
6020 RETURN
```

PROGRAM REPORTS (continued)

5

TESTING AND VERIFICATION

When a program has been written, debugged, and found satisfactory by the programmer, the process of testing and verification begins.

TESTING: AN EXTENSION OF DEBUGGING

When a program is first entered into a computer, it usually contains a few errors which the programmer must find and correct. This process was described in Chapter 4 and is known as debugging. These errors are found by the programmer and are corrected based on the programmer´s assumptions about how the specification detailed the program. Errors usually involve such details as:

1. Instructions the computer cannot decode
2. Incorrect syntax of computer instructions
3. Typographical errors such as the omission of an instruction or mis-typed instructions
4. Incorrect implementation of an algorithm
5. Incorrect algorithms

The last error is usually the most troublesome, since the program does not solve the problem described in the specification.

Although it is much like debugging, testing differs in the type of problems that are solved. When a program is ready to undergo testing, the programmer feels that it is operating correctly according to his interpretation of the specification. The problems that are solved in this step are those that arise when the intended users begin to experiment with the program and request changes. These changes, while they represent software modifications to the program, are not done to eliminate bugs. Instead, most revisions result from an attempt to:

1. Make the program easier to operate. This idea closely relates to the concept of a "friendly" program described earlier. Users may request alterations to reduce

the training time and experience required
to   operate   a program.   Ideally, programs
should provide   helpful   comments   when
necessary. Since documentation of   program
operation   necessary   for the programmer is
contained inside   the   program,   it   should
also contain whatever is   necessary to help
the new operator.

2. Make the program more efficient. The phrase
    "time is money" certainly pertains to   the
    use   of   a computer. In   any organization,
    everyone   wants   to   computerize   each
    function   of   their   department without
    realizing that the computer is not   capable
    of   handling the increased volume. Changes
    made   to   accommodate   this   need   are
    especially valid if   the   program is used
    often or by a large group of users.

3. Protect the   program   from errors. Since it
    is   just   as   easy   to make a   mistake
    executing a program as   it is when writing
    one, modifications   should be   made   to
    protect the program   from bad input data.
    One of   the   more   popular   phrases of
    programmers is,   "Garbage in, garbage out."
    If the program is   not able   to distinguish
    erroneous   data   from   valid data,   the
    results   can   cause   many   headaches.
    Newspapers are   full of stories about   the
    family   that   is   sent   the $100,000.00
    electric   bill or   the man   who   receives a

letter informing him that he is deceased.
It is desirable to have the computer catch
as many errors as possible before they
become permanent record and complicate the
solution.

4. Increase the security of the program. Some
   programs must include the feature that
   only specific users can gain access to the
   program. This type of security is usually
   accomplished by password protection and
   record keeping that details what users
   executed the program and when. Protection
   may also take the form of making sure that
   valuable records are not destroyed or
   altered in any way.

5. Accommodate changes that are not included
   in the specification. During program
   development, users may have second
   thoughts about the specification and may
   ask to insert additional features.
   Although ideally the programmers should be
   informed of this decision as soon as
   possible, users tend to make their desires
   known only when they begin to use the
   program for the first time. While this
   policy can get to be very frustrating, the
   programmer may be forced to comply with
   these requests in order to get the program
   released.

Another type of modification occurs
when the specification itself is wrong.
Modifications must be made before the
program can even begin to be retested by
the users. Again, the importance of a
clear, concise, and complete specification
is obvious. Since a programmer cannot "do
what I mean, not what I say," the
programmer must rely on the information
contained in the specification, using a
minimum amount of interpretation.

While this list is not comprehensive, it does
outline the major reasons why testing and
verification take place. It should now be clear
that the emphasis on error correction shifts from
programming to user response and interaction. With
this viewpoint in mind, we now proceed to define
the steps taken in the verification/test process.

First, the program must be compared to the
specification in a variety of areas to ensure that
the program fulfills its intended purpose. Any
changes made for one of the above reasons (or any
other reason) should be coded, debugged, and
verified again before proceeding any further. When
this process is over, the user and programmer
should both be satisfied that all functional
requirements are met. The program is then
considered ready for release from a functional
point of view.

The program must then undergo testing under a defined procedure that ensures the integrity of the software. Since its function is now fixed, emphasis is placed on making sure the program includes many desirable characteristics not related to the program's function. Following completion of this step, the program is ready for release.

COMPARISON TO THE SPECIFICATION

The most obvious test that can be done on a program is a check to see that it correctly performs its intended function. Since a program is useless if it solves the wrong problem, this is the first step in the testing/verification process. Throughout the design process, the specification is used to gain information that determines the content and organization of software. Now the specification is used to see how well the program measures up to the design goal.

Comparison with the specification should take place with the users and programmers present. Sample runs should be executed and evaluations should be made based upon the program's functional ability. Any areas of dissatisfaction should be modified and then rechecked to make sure they are correct. Although there are other areas of evaluation, verification should take place in these major areas:

1. Functionality. Every operation included in the program must be checked to make sure

the program functions in the desired
manner. Sample data sets are entered and
the results are checked to see that the
data has been correctly processed. This
usually requires the most time, since the
entire program is scanned and evaluated.

2. Completeness. Every operation detailed in
    the specification must appear in the
    program. When testing for functionality,
    it is suggested that those verifying the
    program "check off" each function as it is
    encountered. In this way, the scope of the
    program can be verified and functions
    which were omitted can be found.

3. Data formats. Data that is entered, stored,
    and processed must be done in a way that
    makes it easy to retrieve. Make sure that
    data is kept in the proper files and
    stored in a logically correct sequence.

    Other formats of concern come from
those used to display information back to
the user. Terminal displays should be
organized, uncluttered, and easy to
understand. Charts and graphs should have
appropriate labels, scales, and units.
Reports should be neat and well organized,
with straight columns and wide margins.
Longer reports should have numbered pages
and the data created so that they are not
confused with earlier printouts. In short,

any output that a user comes in contact
with should be visually appealing and
organized so that information can be
easily found. The use of reverse video,
upper and lower case letters, underlining,
and flashing displays will greatly enhance
the readability of computer output.

4. Operator interface. The program should
    prompt the user in some standard format
    whenever data is to be entered, decisions
    made, or instructions performed. Operator
    response should be as short as possible
    and must be checked for errors. If errors
    do occur, the program should detail them
    completely enough for the operator to make
    corrections. In an input process function,
    the program should allow the user the
    option of starting over or cancelling what
    was entered and terminating the function.
    Each of these "finishing touches" allows
    the operator to interact with the computer
    more effectively and efficiently.

TESTING

When the program has been functionally verified,
the programmer can proceed with the testing
process. Tests are conducted in a wide range of
areas to make sure the program is ready for
release. Thorough testing of a program will reveal
certain characteristics, which may or may not be
desirable.

One of the best characteristics a program can
have is resistance to failure. This prevents the
program from crashing, destroying parts of itself,
or parts of the data storage it uses. This type of
program is able to spot and point out erroneous
input data, report this fact to the user, and then
request new data. If required peripheral devices
such as a printer or disk drive are missing or not
active, the program detects this and aborts further
processing until they are ready. Finally, if an
error does occur, the program should shut down in
an orderly fashion so it protects itself and the
stored data.

Programs of this type are known as
"bullet-proofed," "protective," or "defensive"
programs. However, the program does not get this
characteristic on its own. The programmer must
determine the uses and abuses that will take place
inside the program and take action accordingly to
protect it. This type of protection is well worth
the additional time required in design and testing,
as loss of the program or data can cause
large-scale problems when the program is used
heavily or interacts with others using a common
data storage.

Testing must also be done to ensure that the
programs communicate with peripheral devices in an
efficient manner. Keyboards, displays, printers,
tape and disk drives, and links to automated
equipment should all be included in the testing
process where applicable. These external devices

play an important part in supplying the computer with the input/output channels it uses to send information. Good programs have the characteristics that they correctly use each device quickly and efficiently and interpret the information that is returned to them.

It is also useful for programs to have self-test features. These self-tests may be monitored continuously or could be invoked by the user. Self tests usually check the computer and peripheral hardware to make sure they are "up and running." Checks may also be performed on the stored data to make sure nothing has been destroyed or altered. Self-test characteristics may not be applicable in every program, but they are useful when the computer must monitor itself so that it can be taken for granted that the system is functioning correctly.

Since it is impossible to test a program completely, tests must be chosen to cover the widest possible scope of the program. Bergland (1) says that testing "does not verify correctness. It simply raises your confidence." Submit programs to enough testing that you have enough confidence to release them. In addition, cover these major areas:

1. Test end conditions. Make sure that each loop executes the correct number of times and terminates properly on the last loop. Check counters, indices, and offsets that are incremented or decremented to see that

they count up or down to their maximum or
minimum values.

2. Test special conditions. Make sure that
special case input is handled correctly
and that every error that responds with a
message is simulated. This particularly
pertains to supplying incorrect data at
the input. Other examples would be
checking for a zero divisor before
division or a negative number before
taking the log or square root.

3. Print data and values of variables to make
sure the program is performing the correct
functions. It is also useful to insert
messages during the test phase that notify
the programmer as to what part of the
program has been completed or is presently
being executed.

In addition to the above, it may be useful to check
the following through a series of test:

4. Wherever the program tests conditions and
then branches to a different part of the
program, run sample data that determines
that the program correctly computes the
condition and the proper branch location.
For example, in an IF X = 0 THEN ...
statement, see that data is run where the
result X becomes zero and nonzero. It is
easy to find these statements by reviewing

the flow charts and searching for the
decision diamonds and program flow arrows.

5. Send flawed data to each subroutine and see
    how it recovers. Some may return with
    programmed error messages or cause the
    program to cease execution, returning
    control to the computer's operating system
    or monitor. Since loss of control may not
    be permissible, each subroutine should be
    checked so that execution errors cannot
    occur.

6. If the program has security features, test
    to determine what measures must be taken
    to circumvent this security. Pay
    particular attention to statements that
    protect the program from unauthorized
    modifications.

7. Verify from long - term testing that the
    program runs reliably and consistently,
    producing the same results every time for
    the same input. Problems can result when a
    program begins to write over itself after
    running for long periods of time. It is
    also possible that certain sequences of
    events, found usually by trial and error,
    can cause the program to fail. Programs
    should be given time to "burn in" like
    their hardware counterparts.

8. Test degenerate cases for the program´s
    inputs to each module. Check to see what
    happens if input files or variables are
    empty and have an undefined or
    indeterminate value. Also check to see
    what happens when very large files are
    used, as the computer program may not have
    sufficient temporary storage to
    accommodate them.

A combination of these tests will offer
assurance that the program is ready for release and
can handle many of the foreseeable errors that
could occur. It should be emphasized that it is
much easier to detect and correct errors before the
program is released than after it is in use.
Therefore, any extra attempts to ensure that the
program arrives to its users without errors should
be considered when time permits.

With these areas in mind, testing can begin in
one of two ways. The entire program can be entered
into the machine and tested by running through all
of the program´s function. It is also possible to
test each module separately, with fewer tests run
when the entire program is checked and pieced
together. The second method is usually preferred
because the programmer can focus on a particular
area and look for problems rather than concentrate
on the program as a whole. This is much the same
argument that was presented for modular debugging.

SUMMARY

Testing and verification represent an extension of
the debugging process. This step assures that the
program operates according to the specification and
that   the   user   is   satisfied   with   the   results.
Comparison to the specification is the only valid
way to measure software correctness, as this is the
only source for information about how the program
is to operate.

     Following completion of the verification of
correctness, the programmer should test the program
to   determine   its   characteristics   under   error
conditions. Tests are conducted in a variety of
areas to ensure that the program is able to
pinpoint and respond to errors that it encounters.
This characteristic is known as "bullet proofing" a
program and is very useful in preventing accidental
damage to the program or memory. This ensures a
reliable program that will protect itself when
erroneous data is inputted or computed during
execution of the program.

REFERENCE

1. G. D. Bergland,   A Guided Tour of Program
    Design Methodologies   , Computer, October 1981,
    p. 17.

6

SOFTWARE PERFORMANCE

When the program is written, debugged, tested, and verified, the brunt of the software development effort is over. The final phase of program development is the documentation phase. At this time the program is described by its performance characteristics. Operator manuals are then compiled based on this description so the user can understand how the program operates. In addition, the program is reviewed for the last time in an attempt to optimize it to run most efficiently.

SOFTWARE DESCRIPTION KEYWORDS

Just as the specification was the guiding tool for
the construction and development of a program, the
performance characterization is the main source of
operator information. This description of
performance should outline to the user how the
program operates.

Performance characteristics should be
described by analyzing the program in a variety of
areas. Each area is then rated separately from the
others to give a clear picture of the total
program. These areas are known as software
descriptive keywords and are a standard checklist
that should be used whenever written documentation
is prepared. Most of these keywords pertain to
certain characteristics of individual modules
within the program. The evaluation of the whole
program is then accomplished by looking for a trend
or style common to most of the modules.

The next few paragraphs detail a brief listing
of some of the areas where performance should be
reviewed. The first several pertain mostly to
modules within the program while the latter ones
can be evaluated by reviewing the program as a
whole.

It is possible to have a program module that
is called many different times from numerous
locations inside the program. This module has the
characteristic of a wide "fan-in." Yourdan and

Constantine (1) define fan-in of a module as "the number of superordinate modules that call upon it." In general, wide fan-in is a desirable trait in a program because the program then uses only one module to implement a function. This is preferred to having several modules which do the same thing except for small differences. These differences can usually be consolidated so that one module does the work of many. Examples of high fan-in modules include input/output drivers that interface with CRT terminals and sorting routines. However, there are instances where high fan-in is accomplished by generalizing the module to such a degree that it no longer performs its function effectively. The programmer must decide how far he can go to accommodate fan-in without increasing the size or complexity of his modules to any great extent.

While fan-in was concerned with the number of modules able to enter a given module, attention should be focused on the module exit as well. The term "fan-out" refers to the number of modules a given module can "feed" into based on the data that was processed. Small fan-outs are undesirable because they usually contain too many functions that require special inputs and outputs. With a fan-out of one, the module may be chained into the module it fans out to, thereby decreasing the number of modules and some of the code that goes with both. High fan-outs can be just as bad because they indicate too few of the program's functions are grouped together. In addition, high fan-outs make it difficult to determine where the program

continues as it exits the module. Again, the choice
of how many modules in the fan-out depends on the
programmer.

    It is also desirable to have modules that
relate to one another, picking up where the last
one left off and sending the new results to the
next module. Modules which fit together in this
manner exhibit a high degree of "coupling," which
is defined by Bergland (2) as "a measure of the
strength of interconnection between modules."
Modules which are not coupled together at all are
called "independent," because they do not require
the process of the other to perform their function.
Good programs are normally comprised of modules
which are independent as well as coupled. Coupling
has the advantage that each module is permitted to
process the inputted data and produce new results
for the next module in an assembly line fashion.
However, imagine what happens to the assembly line
when, somewhere along the way, a piece is left out
or is installed incorrectly. Attempts to build
further on that piece can cause many other related
parts to have problems. Such is the case with
modules that are closely coupled. Unless data is
passed between modules correctly, errors will be
magnified as they go from one part of the program
to the next. Independent modules suffer less from
this problem but may contain repetitive code that
is carried throughout other modules. This
repetition is a waste of computer time and memory
and is less efficient than close coupling. Programs
which contain excessive amounts of either of these

two types of modules should be avoided. Proper implementation of coupling allows a minimum of parameter passing between modules and minimizes the amount of code that must be repeated in several modules.

It is also necessary to define how well the statements inside a module are grouped together to form that module. A measure of how well a module is held together is known as the "cohesion" of the module. Cohesion defines the extent that processing statements group together to form the function that defines the module. Seven levels of cohesion have been defined by Constantine (3) based on the association between statements within a module.

The lowest level of cohesion occurs in modules where statements are grouped together by coincidental association. At this level the statements in a module are thrown together without the existence of any relationship between them. Modules of this type have little or no "glue" holding them together and statements can be easily separated from each other and put elsewhere.

The next level of cohesion described modules whose statements are grouped by logical association. These statements are grouped together because they perform nearly the same function. This is very different than the random grouping of statements found in coincidental association. An example of logical association is a set of error messages consolidated into a single error module.

Although they may be different messages, each performs the same logical function of notifying the operator of an error.

When a set of operations are grouped together because they must execute in the same time frame, cohesion results due to temporal association. These statements are linked to each other because they must all be executed at essentially the same time. For example, the statement that turns the red light off in the east/west direction of a traffic light could be linked to the statements which turn the east/west green light on, turn the north/south red light on, and turn the east/west pedestrian walk light on. Although these actions may be implemented in several statements, an observer will note that they all happen at about the same time.

Cohesion can also occur when several functions are grouped together in one module as part of a process. These statements are grouped together by procedural association. If we refer back to flowcharts, the rectangles which have several operations in them could comprise one module with statements that are grouped by procedural association. A module could then be composed of all steps between decision diamonds, with the program control arrows directing operation to a different module or to a point inside the first module.

When a program uses data sets, the statements that use a common source of data should all be grouped together. This grouping by common data represents another type of cohesion caused by communicational association. Statements in the example program that modified and stored the data in the membership file were grouped together using communicational association. This type of cohesion is found primarily where accesses are made to a fixed data base and in modules that handle data which is supplied from the input/output routines.

Sequential association is a source of cohesion in modules that operate in the assembly line fashion described earlier. These modules develop cohesion due to coupling between other modules and themselves. A grouping of statements is characterized by accepting data from another source (usually another module), modifying it in some manner, and passing the results along to a new destination (again, usually another module).

The highest form of cohesion occurs when each statement provides a part in accomplishing one function that comprises the entire module. Such statements are grouped together within a module by the bond of functional association. This module provides only one function, but contains all the necessary instructions required to implement the algorithm of the function. This is the best type of cohesion, as the statements are bound together as tightly as possible. It is also the primary justification for assigning each module only one function and then developing the instructions which will implement it.

The highest degree of cohesion should be maintained wherever possible, so that all modules are well organized and bound closely together. Whenever possible, modules should be grouped together using communicational, sequential, and functional association to keep the level of cohesion high. Such well grouped modules are easier to understand and modify should a new programmer see them for the first time.

PORTABILITY

The characteristic of portability is important enough to belong in a class by itself. Recall from an earlier definition that portability is the characteristic that allows a program to run on various computers with little or no software changes. Since a portable program has a much larger number of potential users, this characteristic can be a great asset when marketing programs.

Several steps must be followed to make a program portable. First, the program must be written in a language that is standardized over a wide range of computer equipment. To assist in this area, many engineering organizations and professional societies are writing specifications to standardize computer languages. These specifications outline the standard instruction set and features that make up a working language. Then programs can be written using these statements with complete portability among all users of the same language.

Another step in portability involves the
design of modules within the program. Since
machine-to-machine compatibility is required, parts
of the program that interact with specific hardware
in the computer should be grouped into separate
modules, known as drivers. Typical drivers usually
control the input/output units as well as other
peripheral devices. A program can then be made
portable by changing the drivers to accomodate
different machines. These changes are usually much
simpler than re-writing the entire program, since
new drivers can usually be written based on the
HIPO block description outlined at the start of the
module.

The same problem with interfacing to the
hardware through drivers can also be present in
interfacing to the operating system software of the
computer. Operating system dependancies must
therefore be isolated into other drivers, just as
the hardware dependancies were. These routines are
used to work with the file formatting structure of
the operating system, so that the method used to
store data on devices like disk drives is
transparent to the programmer and the user.

A final point to consider is the amount and
scope of information that is provided to the user.
If new drivers are required for different
computers, enough programming information should be
supplied so another programmer can understand what
each driver must do. It may be useful to supply
several drivers compatible with many machine and

operating systems and let the user insert the correct one. In either case, more information should be provided to the user than a standard operator´s manual. The programmer should also be prepared to provide software support to these users to achieve compatibility between the program and their system.

The general rule of program portability is to standardize as many of the variables connected with computer programming as possible. As illustrated, this includes the choices of languages and operating systems. Any remaining variables should be separated from the rest of the program and formed into modules. The modules should then be clearly defined so that others can be written to perform the same function and maintain program compatibility. Extensive documentation goes hand-in-hand with these modules so that conversion will be as easy as possible.

OPERATOR AND INSTRUCTION MANUALS

Throughout the software design process, the programmer has been keeping documentation on the program in the form of a project workbook. As progress was made through the different design phases, information was added to bring the program up to date. The program should then be ready for filing with the software librarian at the end of the software performance step. When the program is filed, it should include the project workbook, since this provides all the information about the

design and development of the software. At filing
time, the project workbook contains:

1. The original specification that outlines
    the intent of the program

2. Flow charts or psuedo-code representations
    of each module in the program

3. The source code representations of each of
    the modules

4. Any additional documentation that goes with
    the source code (HIPO documentation blocks
    and self documentation should be provided
    in the source code listings)

5. Brief descriptions of errors encountered in
    the debugging process and what was done to
    correct those problems

6. Brief descriptions of tests conducted on
    the software during the verification
    process and the results of those tests

7. An outline of the software´s performance
    characteristics based upon the keywords
    described earlier

    This manual is far too comprehensive for an
operator´s manual and may even provide more
information about the program than you are willing
to disclose! The operator´s manual should not be

prepared for a programmer but should instead gear itself to the individual who will operate the program on a day-to-day basis. This requires a new type of documentation package that assists the user in getting started and maintaining the program once it is used on a regular basis.

The first few pages of any good documentation package contain a brief description of what the program can do. All basic functions and options should be outlined. Any system requirements (such as machine type or memory size) should be expressed. Special features that separate this program from others should also be included. In this way, a prospective user can read the first few pages of the manual and determine if this program has a potential application that interests him.

The next few pages should illustrate how the program is executed and set up with initial values. It is helpful to cover all the necessary procedures from turning the computer on to completing the program start-up and initialization phase. Illustrations of screen formats that occur in various parts of the program serve to guide the new user through each function of the program. Another simple approach explains what the user should type and then what results the program sends back. This type of hands-on training is a great help in informing users. The program itself should contain many of the instructions and should guide the user through the program. In-depth explanations about each function and option illustrated in the first

part of the package should be included as they are
presented in the training exercises.

Additional information should be provided
about error messages. Since most error messages are
abbreviated to save memory space, explanations of
these errors are provided in the documentation.
Trouble shooting charts should be available that
list probable causes for errors and methods of
correction. In no case should an error exist that
causes complete failure in the system, even though
the documentation includes warnings about this
occurrence. Documentation of this type only acts as
a catalyst in the scenario where users do
everything possible to bring this error condition
about and then berate the programmer for "defective
software." Again, the concept of a "bullet proof"
program is a valid one.

The rest of the documentation package can be
secured from the project workbook, with minor
alterations to make the information readable to
someone outside the software group. Just as most
hardware manufacturers include schematic diagrams
of their electrical circuit designs, the programmer
should include a complete listing of the program in
the documentation package for operators. Additional
software documentation should also be included,
especially if the users will be required to alter
drivers to get the program running on their
computer. Some of the software performance review
can also be used as an effective performance
summary, appearing in the first few pages in the

general description section of the operator´s
manual.

Since engineers are notorious for poor
spelling and sentence structure (this author is no
exception), it is best to enlist the help of a
competent technical writer when preparing the
operator´s manual. It may also be possible to turn
that phase of the project over to the first users
who assisted in the verification/testing process,
having them prepare the training sequence based on
their own experience. The programmer would then
assist by supplying all the necessary information
and reading the manuscript to make sure that the
sequences used in the training exercises are
correct.

OPTIMIZATION BY REVIEW

The final step in program development is
optimization of the entire program. This also
serves as a final review before the program is
released with its documentation. Here the
programmer scans through the entire program,
searching for ways to improve the software without
major alterations or affecting other parts of the
program.

Optimization can be thought of as a step where
performance is improved without making sweeping
changes in the program´s content. Improvements can
be made in a wide range of areas to make the
program faster, more efficient, and easier to use.

The most familiar area of optimization concerns improvements made to improve the program's operation within the computer. Modules should be reviewed to make sure their coding does not waste memory space within the machine. Alternates should be used if they free up additional memory, as this leaves room for future expansion. This may allow users who have computers with smaller memory sizes the chance to implement the program. Each routine should also be checked to see that they execute in the quickest possible time. This is particularly important when programs are operating on a computer system that allows many users to execute their programs simultaneously. As a general rule, programs using minimal memory also tend to execute quickly since there are fewer instructions to fetch, decode, and execute. Likewise, optimization of execution time results from the elimination of instructions, which also reduces the memory size of the program. Since these two areas are so closely related, it is best to optimize these two areas at the same time.

An additional concern for optimization focuses on the efficient allocation and control of the computers resources such as peripheral devices. Programs should be reviewed for ways to keep all devices required by the program busy whenever possible, or to turn them over to other users on the system when they are idle. For example, most personal computers have routines that send characters to a line printer for hard copy printout. A typical output driver for this printer

operates in the following manner. The printer is
first checked to see if it is ready to receive a
character. If it is busy or has been turned off,
the computer waits and keeps checking to see if the
printer is ready. When the printer responds, the
computer sends the character to be printed to the
printer and repeats the cycle. Suppose the printer
is able to receive 100 characters every second.
Since the computer sends the characters to the
printer in one instruction, this takes very little
time. As a result, the computer must then wait
almost 1/100 second until the printer is ready
again. It is not uncommon for some computers to be
able to execute ten thousand machine cycles in that
period of time! Obviously, the computer is not
being used very effectively during this wait.
However, it is possible to alter this type of
program so that the computer executes useful
instructions during this time period, returning to
the line printer driver only when the printer is
ready for the next character. This is a great
improvement in speeding up the program and it also
helps keep both devices busy doing something
useful. The programmer should look for areas where
one device must wait on another one and try to
remove the bottlenecks. In this way, every device
is ready when the computer accesses it and is busy
processing the computer´s instructions when it is
busy accessing another device.

Other bottlenecks can occur when various
modules play a more important role in the program
than others do. Some modules may be used hundreds

of times during a single part of a program, while
others are used only once or twice. Critical
routines should therefore be located, and
optimization of these routines should be of highest
priority. These routines can be re-coded using more
efficient algorithms or a more efficient language.
As a last resort, the routines could be recoded
directly into the computer's assembly language,
bypassing all overhead losses due to use of a
high-level language.

Attempts can also be made to speed up the time
taken for an operator to respond. A simple approach
to this problem informs the user of the options
available at a particular point in the program and
assigns a number or letter to correspond with each
option. The user can then select the desired option
by choosing the correct letter or number, rather
than running a separate program or typing in a
longer response. Another way to reduce response
time is with function keys. This technique picks
several keys on the keyboard and relates special
functions to them consistant throughout the entire
program. For example, the escape key (ESC) could be
used to erase an incorrect response to a question
so that the question will be asked again. The break
key normally stops executing the program and causes
the computer to return to the operating system or
monitor. The computer can also guess at the correct
answer, print it, and have the user merely press
the return key if the answer is correct. Examples
of this occur when the machine assumes the correct
date to put on reports is the current date, even

though the option to use another date is permitted. Still another approach lets the user configure the program to suit the application, processing information according to this configuration without requiring additional information from the user.

In all these techniques, the objective is to minimize the number and length of responses the operator must make to keep the program supplied with input data. Whenever possible, the program should perform its operations without requiring outside data or supply its own data based on an initial configuration. This keeps the computer busy processing rather than waiting for an operator response.

SUMMARY

The performance evaluation represents the final step in the software design process. The finished program is characterized according to a list of descriptive keywords to define how the program functions. Many of the performance keywords relate to the program's functioning on a modular level, so that a description of the entire program is done by observing trends throughout the modules. Final documentation is then prepared to serve two distinct groups. The project workbook is brought up to date, so that it is an accurate, thorough source of information for all programmers who may later be involved with the program. This manual is filed with the software librarian along with a copy of the program for permanent storage. A second manual is then prepared using information from the project workbook and additional references. This manual is geared for the users and operators and contains training and operations information. It may also contain information of a technical nature when programs must be user modified to achieve portability. Following completion of both manuals, the programmer reviews the software one final time, looking for ways to improve the performance of the program. This optimization review focuses on ways to make the program more understandable by both the computer and the operator.

The end result of the structured program design process is a modularized, well-coded program that fulfills the needs set down in the specification. It is virtually error-free and requires a minimum of advance information to operate. It reacts with the user in a friendly manner, pointing out errors and taking steps to correct them. If changes are required or additions are to be made, the program is well documented from both outside and within so that alterations are simple and can maintain the same structure as the original program. Finally, the documentation, program, and reference material are put on file in a convenient place so that other programmers have access to these resources.

REFERENCES

1. Edward Yourdon and Larry L. Constantine, Structured Design - Fundamentals of a

Software Performance

Discipline of Computer Program and Systems
Design , Prentice-Hall, 1979, pp. 171 - 174

2. G. D. Bergland, A Guided Tour of Program
Design Methodologies , Computer, October
1981, page 16

3. Edward Yourdon and Larry L. Constantine,
Structured Design - Fundamentals of a
Discipline of Computer Program and Systems
Design", Prentice-Hall, 1979, pp. 108 - 130

OPERATOR'S MANUAL FOR THE MEMBERSHIP PROGRAM

A. Introduction

This operating manual details how to use the membership record program. Step-by-step instructions are provided to guide the user through each option of the program. This program was designed to keep track of information common to most clubs and organizations. Membership data can be kept on file for eacn member, and this information can be used for various printouts and mailings. This simplifies the process of record keeping for each member.

The program is divided into two main parts, a part which handles each member's information, and a part that prints out various lists and letters. These two parts allow you to add, delete, and update the information kept on file for each club member. This information can then be printed out in various forms for use as membership lists, mailing lists, and payment lists. In addition, several form letters are provided to inform members of the next meeting and when it is time to pay dues.

Instructions are provided for this program showing how each part operates. You will first learn how to enter, change, and remove information on each member. Following this, a description of how to use each of the printout functions is provided.

B. Getting Started

Never use the original copy of this program for a
membership list! Create two backup copies of this
program disk and use them instead, as your original
should be kept in a safe place. This disk is also
sent with the write protect tab in place,
preventing accidental erasure of the program. For
help in how to make backup copies, please consult
your operator´s manual.

To start the program, do the following steps:

1. Turn on the computer and other devices.
2. Insert the program disk into disk drive 0.
3. Press RESET on the computer.

The program will load automatically and the main
menu should appear on the screen. If this does not
occur, the disk may be defective. Try a different
one and see if it works. If it does not, the
computer may be malfunctioning. Check your
operator´s manual for instructions on testing your
computer or calling service personnel.

When the main menu appears, you will be
presented with three choices. To add, change, or
delete data in the master membership file, select
Option 1. To get a printout of one of the five
lists or letters, use Option 2. If you wish to exit
the program, use Option 3. Simply enter your
selection and press ENTER.

C. Record Keeping

The record keeping option is selected by choosing Option 1 from the main menu. This option lets you keep up to date information on each member in the master membership file.

When you select Option 1, the screen clears and a new menu is presented. This menu contains the four record keeping options available. Option 1 allows you to add a new member's information into the master membership file. Option 2 lets you change the information currently stored in the master membership file for a particular member. Option 3 allows you to delete all information on a member from the master membership file. Option 4 exits this menu and returns to the main menu.

1. Add Member Option

To add information about a new member into the master membership file, use Option 1. This is the Add Member option, and the program will automatically open up file space for the new member's data. The program then begins to prompt you for the information required for each member in the organization.

The computer will first ask for the member's name. Type in the member's name by entering the last name, a space, the first name, another space, and the middle initial. You may use up to 30 characters. Use the RUBOUT key if you make a mistake while typing. When you have entered the name correctly, press ENTER. The program will put the name on the screen next to the heading NAME. Do not use commas between each part of the name, as the computer will ignore all characters that follow the first comma.

Next, enter the address by typing in the street number, a space, and the street name. You may again use up to 30 characters. Press ENTER when you have finished, and the address should appear under the name.

You may then enter the city, state, and zip code using up to 20 characters. Type in the city followed by a space, the state, another space, and the zip code. Press ENTER when you are done.

Now enter the date the member joined the organization. There are 8 characters reserved for this, and several formats are acceptable. The most common conventions are:

MM-DD-YY or
MM/DD/YY

Other combinations are permissible providing they use 8 characters. Press ENTER to store the data.

Dues status is used to determine if the member has paid his yearly dues. Enter a "Y" if the dues have been paid, and an "N" if they have not. Press ENTER to store the dues status.

Finally, enter the member´s phone number by
typing the area code, a "-" sign, the first three
digits, another "-" sign, and the last four digits.
Press the ENTER key to store the phone number.

After you have entered all this information
about your new member, review it closely. The
program now gives you three choices. If the
information is correct and you would like to file
it, select Option 1. If you have made an error and
want to re-do the information, select Option 2 and
repeat all of the above instructions from the
beginning. If you wish to cancel the data you have
typed in and exit the Add Member option, select
Option 3.

2. Change Member Option

Once information about a member is stored in the
master membership file, it may need to be updated
periodically. Changes such as a new address, phone
number, or dues status can be done through the
Change Member option. This option is used when you
select Option 2 from the record keeping menu.

To begin changing a member´s information, you
must specify the record number in the master
membership file where this information exists. You
can obtain this number from the membership list
printout. After you enter this number, the data
available on that member is displayed on the
screen.

The   program will then prompt   you   for changes
to the name, address, membership date, dues status,
and phone number. Enter your changes using the same
formats detailed in the Add Member option. If you
do not wish to change a particular piece   of
information, press the ENTER key and the program
will skip to the next item. As you make changes,
the   revised information will   replace the old
information on the display screen.

After you have finished entering the data for
a   particular member, the program   allows   two
options. If you have made a mistake or have changed
the wrong member´s data, you can cancel those
changes and exit this option. If your corrections
are accurate, you can file the changes away and go
on to another member, or exit this option.

3. Delete Member Option

Over a period of time, members may become inactive
or cease to be involved in your organization.
Option 3, the Delete Member option, allows you to
remove the information of such members from the
master membership file. The file is then compressed
to save disk space, and new membership numbers are
assigned. Consequently, it is advisable to
terminate the records of inactive members only once
a year. See the Report Printout section of this
manual for information on how to print a membership
list.

To begin the process of deleting a member's
record, you must first specify that member's record
number in the master membership file. The program
will then sort through the file and find the
appropriate record. As a confirmation, the name of
the member will be displayed and the program will
ask if this is the correct record. If you want to
delete this record, type a "Y," otherwise type an
"N." If you instructed the program to delete this
record, the master file will then be re-organized
and copied back to the disk. This process takes
some time for a disk with many members, so do not
worry if the program appears to be slowing down.
When you have finished deleting members, press
ENTER instead of typing in a member's number in
order to return to the record keeping menu.

D. Report Printouts

The Report Printout option is selected by choosing
Option 2 in the main menu. This option uses the
information stored in the master membership file to
print various lists and letters. The output is sent
to a hardcopy device, such as a dot matrix or daisy
wheel printer.

When you select Option 2 from the main menu,
the screen clears and another menu is presented.
This is similar to the record keeping menu
described earlier. This menu contains the six
report printout options available. Option 1 prints
a membership list of all members and their member

number. Option 2 prints a list of all members who
have not yet paid their dues. Option 3 prints
mailing labels for each member. Option 4 prints a
letter announcing the next meeting and giving
details about its time and place. Option 5 prints a
form letter to a member advising him that he must
pay his dues. Option 6 exits this menu and returns
to the main menu.

1. Membership List Option

A membership list printout can be obtained by
selecting Option 1 in the report printout menu. No
additonal data is required by the program after
this option is selected. The program will then
print out a list of members from the master
membership file, along with the record number for
each member. The address, city, state, zip code,
phone number, and membership date are also printed.
You will then be returned to the report printout
menu when the printout is completed.

2. Dues List Option

A list of all members who have not paid their dues
is available by selecting Option 2 in the report
printout menu. Again, no additional data needs to
be provided inside this option. The program then
prints the names and record numbers of all members
whose dues status is recorded as not paid. This
option returns to the report printout menu at the
end of the printout.

3. Mailing Label Option

A set of mailing labels can be printed up for those
members stored in the master membership file by
selecting Option 3. The program will then print a
mailing label for each member in the file. Each
label contains the name, address, city, state, and
zip code, and fits on a standard label. Since you
may wish to use special computer paper with
removable labels, the program waits for you to set
up the printer with the correct forms. Turn off the
printer, install the correct forms, and position
the forms so that the print head points to the top
line of a label. Turn the printer back on and press
the ENTER key. The program will then print out the
mailing labels and return to the report printout
menu. You can then change back to standard paper in
the printer.

4. Meeting Announcement Option

A standard form letter is available to notify
members of the next meeting by selecting Option 4.
Before the letter is printed out, you must enter
several pieces of information. The program will
first ask for the location of the meeting. Enter
the name and address of the location followed by
the ENTER key. Do not use commas in this text
string. Next, enter the day and date of the
meeting, again without commas in the text.
Following this, enter the time of the meeting and
remember to include AM or PM. Finally, enter the

main item of business (election of officers, etc.). The resulting form letter will look like this:

Dear Member,

Our next meeting will be held on (date) at (time). We will meet at (location). Our main topic on the agenda is (main business). Hope to see you there!

The last thing the computer will do is prompt for the number of copies desired. Enter the number you want and the program will print them. When it has finished printing, the program returns to the report printout menu.

5. Dues Letter Option

A form letter advising members that they must pay delinquent dues is available by selecting Option 5 from the report printout menu. The program will prompt you for the number of copies of this letter you desire. Enter the number you want and the program will print them. When it has finished printing, the program will return to the report printout menu.

7

MAINTENANCE

The first six chapters of this book have dealt with
design of software using a technique defined as
structured program design. The remainder of this
book will be spent on an area of equal importance -
maintenance. Maintenance is the process whereby old
software is modified to bring it up to date and
fulfill current needs. This process is an on going
one, stopping only when the software is discarded
or replaced by a completely new program.

131

A well-structured program is easily modified to accept changes over its lifetime. Since each function is isolated into a single module, modifications are made by replacing, altering, or removing the functions desired. Time and money are saved because the rest of the program is left alone, so a complete re-write of the program is unnecessary. The emphasis of this process therefore shifts from design of software to design of new modules of software that fit into the existing framework of the program.

This chapter will focus on the types of changes made in the maintenance cycle and the reasons for them. Chapter 8 will then be devoted to the procedure used to process these changes. Again, its step-by step approach closely resembles that of the design and test phases covered in earlier chapters.

ERROR CORRECTION

No matter how many times a program is reviewed, it seems at least one error is found after the software has been released to users. The programmer is then faced with the problem of hunting down the error and correcting it. In addition, the correction should be provided to all present users, and all subsequent releases of the program should include the necessary changes.

Errors can take on many forms. The first (and most easily recognizable) type of error is a failure in program operation. In short, the program does not perform the desired function or it performs it incorrectly. The numerous and rigorous reviews that occur in the structured program design process are there to catch these types of errors. Consequently, it is very unlikely that these errors are present in a program. Many careful reviews minimizes the number of these faults, and the time spent on these reviews is paid back when the programmer is able to catch these errors before a program is released.

Another type of fault cured by maintenance is the logic error, which occurs when the program performs a process in a logically incorrect manner. For example, recall the flowcharting symbols explained earlier in Chapter 3. Decisions were expressed in flowcharts through the use of a diamond shaped symbol, a test condition, and program control flow arrows that showed where the program continued depending upon the result of the test. A logic error occurs when an error is found in any one of these areas. The test condition can be in error if it tests a condition that always has one value, so that the program never branches to the routine that is used for the other conditions. It is also possible that the test is performed on the wrong variables or data, causing what may appear to be random branching after the test.

As an example, look at this program:

```
10 C = 10
20 PRINT "Counter is now ";C
30 C = C - 1
40 IF D = 0 THEN 20
50 END
```

Line 40 contains several errors. To begin
with, where is the Variable D? It is used on the
test condition but nowhere else. Obviously, what
should be tested is the Variable C. The program
then looks like:

```
10 C = 10
20 PRINT "Counter is now ";C
30 C = C - 1
40 IF C = 0 THEN 20
50 END
```

This program is still not correct! The test
condition is reversed, so that the program ends
after printing once for any value other than C = 1.
If we reverse the test condition to make the
program correct, the new program looks like this:

```
10 C = 10
20 PRINT "Counter is now ";C
30 C = C - 1
40 IF C <> 0 THEN 20
50 END
```

Errors can also occur due to misdirection of the branch. For example, a ´yes/no´ or ´true/false´ pair of branches may be reversed, so that the program always picks the wrong choice between two branches. The program could also branch to the wrong location, causing incorrect operation. For example, consider the program:

```
10 C = 10
20 PRINT "Counter is now ";C
30 C = C - 1
40 IF C <> 0 THEN 10
50 END
```

The program has one decision: to test the counter and see if it is zero. If it is zero, the program ends, and we can assume that this is the correct branch path. However, the counter will never decrement to zero because the test for a zero condition branches to the wrong location if the test is false. The statement in line 40 should read:

```
40 IF C <> 0 THEN 20
```

Now the counter decrements correctly and the program executes properly.

These errors usually occur more frequently than do those concerning program operation because the program can never be completely tested. For very large programs, testing of every branch would be impractical. Earlier discussions of flow charts

pointed out that their sole purpose was to
implement the algorithms used in the program in a
logically correct manner. In this way, the
structured program design process again aids in
reducing errors by providing a means for early
detection before the program is released.

Maintenance done on software to correct errors
is the least desirable type because it requires
that revisions be made to all copies presently in
use. Just as automakers are required to recall
their cars when they are delivered to customers
with a potential problem, the programmer is
responsible for supplying a correct program to
users, particularly if they paid for the program.

There are several ways the programmer can
accomplish a software "recall." The easiest way
(for the programmer) is to make the necessary
changes and offer to exchange the new software with
the old version previously in use. Users then
return their old programs and get back new ones
which (hopefully) are now trouble-free. Another
method is to provide a "patch;" a sequence of
statements that corrects the old program. The user
then enters the necessary changes provided by the
patch so that the program works correctly. This is
not desirable because all users must be tracked
down and sent a copy of the patch. Problems can
arise when users, who may have little knowledge of
programming practices, attempt to alter programs
themselves. Whenever possible, a patch should be

provided to programs so that users do not have to
change it themselves.

ENHANCEMENTS AND ADDITIONS

As a program is used over a long period of time,
changes occur in the needs of the user.
Consequently, the program must be adapted to meet
those needs. In addition, feedback from users
returns to the programmer in the form of requests
for new or improved features. The process of
providing improved functions to a computer program
is defined as "enhancement." The process of
supplying new features to a program is known as
"addition." Although closely related, these two
terms are not the same. Enhancements are changes
made to improve the operations of existing
functions. This is similar to the optimization
review explained in Chapter 6. Additions are
changes that implement new functions not previously
included in the program. These changes will require
new algorithms, flow charts, and coded modules.
This represents a repetition of the structured
program design cycle, as design work must be done
to implement new functions.

As mentioned earlier, users provide a large
amount of input concerning program enhancements and
additions. They are continually searching for ways
to get more done in a given amount of time. As a
result, the program is exposed to one long,
continuous optimization review. When the operation
of a program ceases to be productive and effective,

users will be the first to know. Close
communication between the programmer and users can
help in getting changes made when they are needed,
so that the program continues to operate
effectively.

Another source of enhancements and additions
is management. Through the use of surveys,
management can gather new information about the
needs that are present. If these needs dictate a
new program, a specification is drawn up and the
entire structured program design cycle repeats
itself. However, revisions could be made on an
existing program that closely resembles what is
called for. Again, this is much like the first few
steps described in Chapters 2 and 3, where the
programmer receives requests and implements them
into a computer program. The only difference is
that these requests are chained into an existing
program rather than grouped together to form a new
one.

Enhancements and additions are a much more
desirable form of maintenance because they do not
contain the urgency implied in error correction.
The programmer is free to proceed carefully through
the maintenance cycle and design additional
features that add utility to the program. This is
certainly preferred to the rather hectic job of
correcting a program that does not already
function. These changes also allow the programmer
to work on new designs, whether they are brand new

additions or new methods which enhance existing features.

Additions and enhancements can be distributed to users in much the same manner as is done for error correction. The main difference is that the programmer is under no obligation to provide them free of charge. Just as in error correction, additions and enhancements can be obtained on an exchange basis, where users receive new software by turning in their old versions. This allows users to continually upgrade the performance of their programs as new and improved versions become available. However, functions which appear on older versions should be present in new releases. This characteristic is known as upward compatibility, meaning that new versions of a program include all functions of earlier releases plus added features. This ensures that data can be transferred from one version to the next and that operation of the new program does not differ substantially from the earlier release.

Patches can also be provided that include the new features of an improved program. These can be installed into an existing program so that a completely new program source is not required. Patches also ensure upward compatiblity, as the existing data and program are altered very little by the installation of a patch. Since installation by users is still somewhat of a problem (just as it was in error correction), this technique is not foolproof.

THE MAINTENANCE PROCESS

As mentioned earlier, the maintenance process is
very similar to the structured program design
process. Changes made to software are treated much
the same as new programs. The main difference is
that the design of changes must be done so they fit
into an existing program´s structure rather than
become a part of a new program.

The first steps in structured program design
(those of requirements analysis and specification)
have parallels in the maintenance cycle. Before
changes can be made, the type and scope of the
changes must be defined. If too many modifications
must be done to upgrade the program, it may be
easier to begin again and create a new program.
Should the decision be made to modify an existing
program, the programmer must sit down with those
individuals requesting the changes and work out
what needs to be done. Although users are normally
the ones who make such requests, changes can come
from anyone who could request new programs (see
Chapter 2). At the completion of the meeting, a
specification is then drawn up that authorizes
changes made in the program. Such a document is
known as a change notice; its function and content
will be explained further in Chapter 8.

The design phase of maintenance is also
similar to its counterpart in structured program
design. The programmer begins by gathering
resources necessary to make the program

modifications. Since the programmer must work within the existing framework of the program, decisions such as the language choice and design technique (top/down or bottom/up) have already been made. Instead, the programmer secures a copy of the program from the software librarian (the original remains on file) and obtains the project workbook. Information is gathered by reviewing the workbook in order to understand the intent and method of the original program. When the programmer is familiar enough with the program, he constructs flow charts that implement new or enhanced algorithms in the same style as the original. These algorithms represent enhancements or additions to the features presently incorporated into the software, and are detailed in the change notice. A new section in the project workbook also appears that contains all the information to date on modifications. As the maintenance process continues, new material is added to further document the work that is done. Finally, a design review is held to verify the correctness of the changes before coding takes place.

Coding and debugging the changes is the next part in the maintenance cycle. As before, the flow charts are converted into an executable computer language using the structure theorem. However, documentation prepared for maintenance must include more information than its counterpart in the design process. In addition to describing the operation of new or enhanced modules, documentation must also be included that distinguishes them from the original

program. This can be accomplished by using
self-documentation to explain program function, and
then providing additional information in the HIPO
comment block about the enhancements or additions.
When this is completed, a structured walk-through
review can be arranged to check the new software
before it is entered into the machine and debugged.
The modular debugging process varies from the one
used in design because it must now concentrate on
two areas. The first area looks at each new module
to see that it performs the correct function. This
is similar to the debugging procedure used when a
new program is studied for the first time. However,
debugging of changes must also observe what effects
(if any) the new changes have on the existing
modules in the program. It is a common occurrence
to make changes in one part of a program and
unknowingly cause havoc in other sections that are
closely related. Any modules which share data or
variables with a new or modified module should also
be carefully checked to verify that they still
perform properly.

Following completion of the debugging and
coding steps, the program is again turned over to
users for their verification and approval. The
changes are reviewed against the change notice to
make sure every new or enhanced function is
included and operates correctly. When the users are
satisfied with the revisions made to the program,
the programmer begins to subject it to testing.
These tests should concentrate on new or modified
modules so that they will be as thoroughly checked

out as the rest of the program. In addition,
several tests should center on related modules
(just as in the debugging phase) to verify that the
modified parts of the program fit in with the rest.
The end result of these tests should be a program
which is as equally "bullet-proofed" and reliable
as the original.

A new set of performance characteristics is
then drawn up to describe the new version of the
program. The modifications are then subjected to an
optimization review so that they become as
efficient as possible. The documentation that has
been accumulated by the programmer during the
maintenance cycle is then filed with the software
librarian along with a copy of the software. The
problem of user documentation differs slightly from
the design of a new program. If the revisions are
to be sent to users as a "patch" package, new
documentation should be provided to the user about
the modifications. This documentation could then be
added to the existing user's manual to bring the
manual up to data. Should the changes be made
available as a new version of the program, an
updated manual could be created that goes with it,
instead of a manual update. Regardless of which
method is chosen, information must be provided to
users to inform them of any changes that exist in
the operation of the program.

The maintenance design procedure is much like
the structured program design process because both
have similar goals. By following this procedure,

revised   programs   will   continue   to   maintain
desirable   characteristics   in   areas   such   as
modularity,   clarity,   and   efficiency.   A   more
detailed   description   of   some   of   the   topics
presented   here   will   be   provided   in   the   next
chapter.

SERVICING AND TECHNICAL SUPPORT

Two areas   that   are often overlooked in maintenance
are servicing   and   technical support.   These   areas
handle   most   of   the   interaction   with   users   and
should therefore be considered carefully.

    Servicing   refers   to   the   maintenance   and
preservation of software.   This   area generates   the
patches and   revisions needed   for   a   program. When
requests   come   in   from   users,   it is   usually   the
servicing group   that accepts   and then   operates on
them. As   stated   before,   the requests   range   from
correction   of   errors   that   still   exist   in   the
program   to   special   case   modifications.   The
servicing   group   then accepts   these   requests, and
decides whether or not   they will be able to process
them.   If the changes   are   to   be   implemented, the
servicing group   follows   the   maintenance procedure
detailed above and then turns   the   revised software
over to the users.

    Technical support refers to providing   a source
of   information   about   software.   Often   users have
questions about   program operation   or compatibility
between   the   program   and   different   machines.

Technical support provides the answer to these (and
many other) questions through additional
documentation or referrals to other people, such as
the servicing group mentioned above. In addition,
technical support can accumulate information about
problems most frequently encountered by users and
supply this information to programmers or
management. This makes future programs more in line
with user preferences and reduces the number of
problems that occur with new software.

Although only a brief explanation of the
functions of servicing and technical support has
been included here, the importance of these
functions should not be treated lightly. Since both
of these groups work closely with those who need
programs, they are an excellent way to determine
requirements for future programs or new
modifications. With high emphasis placed on meeting
the expectations of users in software designs,
these groups should be consulted so that these
expectations can be more clearly determined.

SUMMARY

Many times a program becomes out of date due to the
changing needs of those who use it. To bring the
program up to date, a procedure is defined to
perform maintenance on existing software.
Maintenance can be needed for a variety of reasons,
but it is usually done to correct errors which were
included in previous releases or to add new or
improved features. A new feature is known as

addition, and a feature which has been improved is
known as enhancement. The maintenance procedure is
very similar to the structured program design
process for designing new software. This is done to
make new portions of the program have the same
style and characteristics as the original.
Individuals who are responsible for using this
process to generate modifications are in charge of
servicing. These modifications are made available
to the user by offering a completely new program
(usually on an exchange or upgrade basis), or by
offering a patch which contains modifications of
specific areas. Other individuals provide
information to the user about the program and are
in charge of technical support. This group may call
on other individuals on a referral basis to provide
answers to many of the questions posed to them by
users.

Again, a structured, well-organized approach
is used to handle this process of maintenance.
Since maintenance is a continuous, long-term cycle,
use of this procedure will aid in keeping the
program well designed and maintainable throughout
its useful life.

8

CONFIGURATION MANAGEMENT

This final chapter will concentrate on some key areas of program maintenance. Emphasis is placed on the documentation required when a program is modified and methods of informing users about modifications.

Configuration management is the term applied to the process of modifying and keeping track of a series of released versions of a software program. As its name implies, each of these programs

represents   a   slightly   different   version   (or
configuration)   of   the   original.   Since   it   is
necessary to keep   information on all existing
versions of the program, some method is required to
manage this information so that it can be easily
accessed. In addition, users must be informed of
the new program revisions and a scheme should be
devised that informs the users about which version
they   are   currently   using.   This   process   was
discussed   in   Chapter   7;   additional   information
about certain areas now follows.

RELEASE, ROLL-OFF, AND ARCHIVE

Programmers should always keep information on every
program   revision. A simple technique that   assures
this information finds its way into   the   project
workbook is   the   release, roll-off, and archive
method. This   technique   begins with the assumption
that the maintenance cycle has been completed and
the modified program is ready to be turned over to
the users.

     The first part of   this technique is the
revision   release. Obviously,   this   means   the
programmer turns over copies of the completed
program or revision to those who install   them on
the computer and execute them. However, additional
material is handed out at this time. Prior to the
release of modified (or new, for that matter)
software, both user and technical documentation is
prepared. As described earlier, the user's manuals
contain a subset of technical information   and

instructions on how to operate the software.
Therefore it is best that the programmer record the
information that will be stored in the software
library first. Following this, the instructions
necessary to use the new program and/or install the
software revisions can be prepared. All this
information can then be given to users at the time
of program release.

The second part of this technique is the
roll-off. In this step, the programmer prepares to
terminate, or roll-off, the project. This
corresponds to the idea of "tying up loose ends"
before a project is successfully concluded. The
information that has been assembled to document the
changes is now collected into one file and
organized. Resources that were collected for
program development are returned so that others can
use them. In short, the programmer collects all
useful data about the modifications made and
compiles it into a presentable form. The process is
now complete, the project is terminated, and the
programmer is free to begin work on other programs.

However, the information obtained on this
project does not sit in some file in the
programmer´s desk. Before beginning a new project,
the programmer should turn over all information to
the software librarian, just as the project
workbook is submitted with a new program. This
information represents a workbook covering a
smaller part of the program that was affected by
the modifications. This represents the final part

of the technique, where the program and its
pertinent data are archived. This permanent storage
is managed by the software librarian so that all
programmers have access to a common source of
information.

    The release, roll-off, and archive method is
an excellent way to get the information obtained
during the maintenance cycle filed away so that
every other programmer can use and benefit from it.
By following this simple technique, the programmer
will prevent the results of his development time
from getting lost before they are needed again.

NOTIFICATION OF REVISION

There are two pieces of information a programmer
must convey to users of a particular program.
First, the programmer must inform a user about new
modifications, so that the revised program can be
distinguished from previous editions. In addition,
the programmer needs to inform users about which
version of the program they have. By using some
means of identification, the programmer is able to
refer back to the information on file for a
particular version of a program in order to answer
questions, make additional modifications, etc.

    Perhaps when you have executed a program or
begun to read its operations manual you have seen
the expression:

> program name VERSION X.Y
> or
> program name VERS. X/Y

This is the way most programmers document the versions of their program. The first number (represented by the letter X) is the major revision level of the program. A new program usually has a major revision level of 1. If for some reason it must be extensively re-written to accommodate many changes, the major revision number is incremented to 2, 3, and so on. A change in the major revision number therefore represents major changes that take place in the program that do not significantly alter the scope or function of a particular program.

The second digit (represented by the letter Y) is the minor revision level. As stated earlier, small changes due to error corrections or additions and enhancements can be installed through the use of a minor revision. When this is done, the minor revision level of the program is incremented by one. New programs which have yet to be modified usually carry a minor revision level of zero.

A delimiter (such as a period, space, hyphen, or a slash) usually appears between the two numbers to separate them. For example, suppose our example membership program is about to be released. It could be called MEMBERSHIP VERS. 1.0. After a year or so new changes are implemented that add features but do not require major re-writes in the program.

The new program would carry the name MEMBERSHIP VERS. 1.1. Subsequent minor revisions would show the version number changing to 1.2, 1.3, 1.4, and so on. Now suppose that the entire program is re-organized to work on a different computer or run under a different language. The program now carries the name MEMBERSHIP VERS. 2.0. Notice that the minor revision level was set back to zero when the major revision level was updated. This was done because there are no minor revisions applied to a program that has just been released under a new major revision level. Subsequent minor revisions that are installed to this major revision would change the number to 2.1, 2.2, 2.3, etc.

This method allows for easy identification of a program from a series of similar versions and provides additional information upon closer examination. Since a minor revision is only used to correct errors or add improved features, a user can expect that all the commands that can be processed on version 1.2 of a program should also be valid on 1.3. This is due to the fact that minor revisions are installed to keep upward compatiblity between minor revision levels. Version 1.3 and 2.0 may not be upwardly compatible because the change represents a change in major revision level. Compatibility is not assured because the scope of the changes is much broader than that of a minor revision.

There are two laws of software defined by Bergland (1) that closely relate to the major

level/minor level type of version identification.
The first is the law of continuing change, which
states:

> A system that is used undergoes continuing
> change until it is judged more cost effective
> to freeze and re-create it.

Simply stated, this means that a program is
constantly revised through the use of software
revisions until it no longer performs its function
effectively. Following this, the program is
re-written, assigned an updated major revision
level, and used as a replacement. The process of
adding minor revisions continues until a new major
revision is once again required.

The second law of software is the law of
increasing unstructuredness, which states:

> The disorder of a system increases with time
> unless specific work is executed to maintain
> or reduce it.

This law states that, over a period of time, the
constant applications of new software revisions
begins to errode the efficiency of the program.
When the software becomes so unorganized that it
loses the advantages obtained by a well structured
program, it is time for a new version to be
created. This "mopping up" operation restores the
software to its original, well-structured form,

thereby gaining back the efficiency and readability it once had.

Use of the two laws aids the programmer in deciding how sweeping those changes must be. When a program becomes so disorganized that it loses the benefits of a structured program, it is no longer cost effective to continue to maintain it and a new revision should be created. Otherwise, the program can be modified by applying a series of minor software revisions and updating the version number accordingly.

CHANGE NOTICE DOCUMENTATION

The first step in software design is the development of a document outlining the intent and purpose of the program. In structured program design, this document is known as a program specification. Chapter 7 outlined the parallel to the specification for the maintenance cycle; it is known as a change notice and its purpose and content will be discussed here.

Change notices are created for the purpose of detailing the required modifications necessary to update a software program. These changes are arrived at by a meeting between programmers and individuals requesting the changes. Modifications which can be implemented using a reasonable amount of resources should be included if they provide additional value or utility to an existing piece of software.

When a change notice is drawn up, it should
contain information concerning the type of change
and the reasons for it. Change notices should
include information on the following items:

1. The date of the change.

2. The software that changes are made on. Be
    sure to include the revision major
    level/minor level of the current version
    of the software.

3. A brief description about why the changes
    are being made. As an example, changes are
    normally made to improve the performance
    of a program, to correct an error, or to
    provide additional functions.

4. A brief description concerning what the
    changes consist of. This description
    should outline which modules are affected
    and should point out what new modules must
    be created.

5. A description of the scope of modification.
    This description should indicate whether
    the changes required will be installed
    with a major or minor program revision.
    This dictates what the next version number
    will be.

6. The individuals who requested the changes.

7. A realistic date of completion based on
certain amounts of manpower and resources.

Much of this information is similar to what
should appear on a new program specification. By
detailing what changes should be done, the change
notice provides a convenient reference about the
type and extent of the modifications that are to be
done to an existing program.

PROBLEM TRACKING DOCUMENTATION

In addition to documenting the changes at the start
of the maintenance cycle using a change notice,
comments should be made as modifications are
developed. This documentation is known as problem
tracking documentation and describes how the
modifications were implemented.

The first part of the maintenance cycle is
documentation of the problem. This is done with a
change notice and is not considered as part of the
problem tracking documentation.

The next step is the assembling of pertinent
data about the program. Problem tracking
documentation begins here by listing the resources
that are required to correct the problem.
Complicated modifications tend to require more
resources than do simple ones because they have
longer development times, tying up computer time as
well as manpower. A description of the amount of

resources used can also indicate just how easy a
particular program can be modified should other
requests come through.

The next step is to find and document the
exact areas where the modifications must be
inserted. In this way, programmers are able to
determine where changes have been inserted in
previous versions of the program so that these can
be reviewed if necessary.

The fourth step of maintenance is the
correction of a backup copy of the original
software. The tracking documentation includes all
new or revised program modules and describes where
they fit into the software. Self documentation is
added to the program statements and a notice of
change is included somewhere (usually at the start)
of each program that refers to a more complete
description of the changes in the problem tracking
documentation.

The final part of problem tracking
documentation contains a listing of the results of
tests that the program undergoes to verify its
correctness. These results should include tests
done on the new or revised modules and modules that
are closely related to the above by common data
sets or variables. Test results yield insight not
only on how well the program functions but also on
how thorough the testing procedure is and how much
of the program it covers.

The final part of maintenance concerns the separate documentation prepared for users about the major or minor revision. It is also not considered a part of problem tracking documentation.

Problem tracking documentation is normally kept in the project workbook and is not provided to users. It does, however, provide a great deal of information about the program modifications and how they were done. This information is essential to other programmers if they should attempt to work on the program at a later date.

SUMMARY

Changes are made in a program using the maintenance cycle described in Chapter 7. A change notice is prepared that acts as a specification for the changes that will be implemented into an existing computer program. Throughout the development process, problem tracking documentation is created that describes how the changes were installed in the program, detailing the history of the modifications. When the program is again ready for release, a new version number is assigned to it that informs the user about the amount of work done on the program and its upward compatibility. Finally, the programmer rolls off, or terminates, the project and files all information with the software librarian for permanent storage.

REFERENCE

1. G. D. Bergland, A Guided Tour of Program Design
    Methodologies , Computer, October 1981, p. 18.

INDEX

For Product Safety Concerns and Information please contact our EU
representative GPSR@taylorandfrancis.com Taylor & Francis Verlag GmbH,
Kaufingerstraße 24, 80331 München, Germany

Printed and bound by CPI Group (UK) Ltd, Croydon, CR0 4YY
08/06/2025
01896998-0016